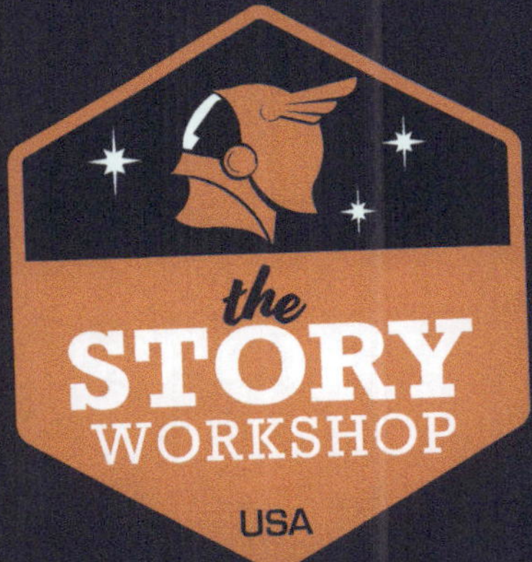
the
STORY
WORKSHOP
USA

THIS BOOK IS FOR
ANYONE WHO WANTS
TO MAKE AND CREATE.

CONTENTS

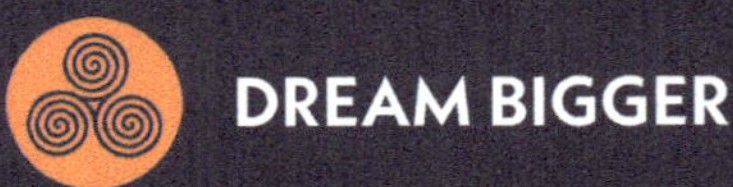

INTRODUCTION
A NEW SINCERITY
09

PHILOSOPHY
CARING AS REBELLION
11

THE MAP & THE COMPASS
HOW TO USE THIS GUIDE
17

WHERE ARE YOU AT?
CREATIVE ERA
19

CHAPTER 01
THE PRIZE INSIDE
23

CHAPTER 02
MEET YOUR MENTOR
33

CHAPTER 03
VISION BOARD IS A MAP
47

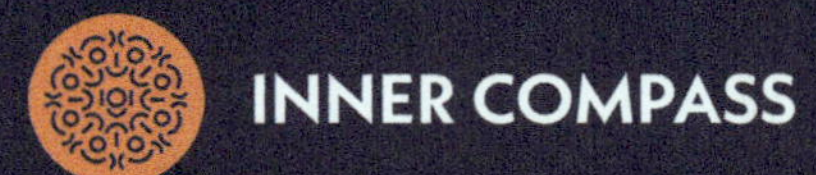

INNER COMPASS

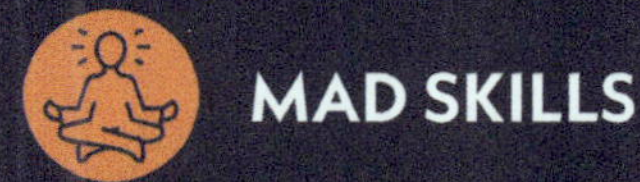

MAD SKILLS

CHAPTER 04
THE FISH POND PRINCIPLE
59

CHAPTER 05
MONSTERS IN DISGUISE
69

CHAPTER 06
EMBRACE YOUR WEIRD
79

CHAPTER 07
STACK THE WINS
91

CHAPTER 08
BUILD YOUR SUPER ROBOT
101

CHAPTER 09
MINING EARLY LOVES
109

CHAPTER 10
RETURN WITH THE ELIXIR
119

CLOSING
CARRY FORWARD
127

WELCOME!

To The Field Guide to Creativity, a hands-on, heart-led workbook to help you on your creative journey. Whether you're reigniting your spark or finding your way forward, this space is yours.

This workbook is both a compass and a playground. Use it to reflect, sketch, write, explore, and build momentum.

There's no wrong way to show up here: JUST START

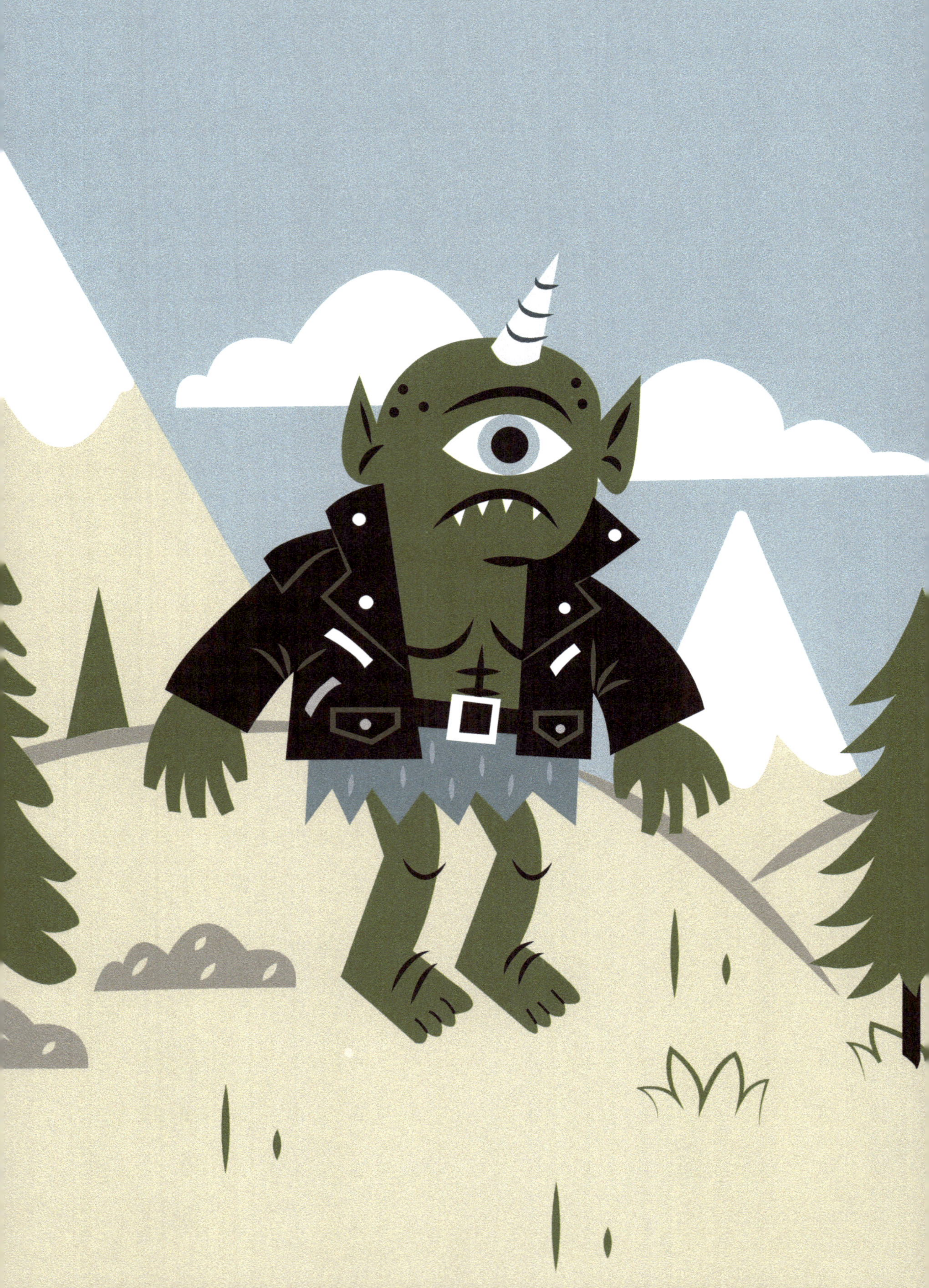

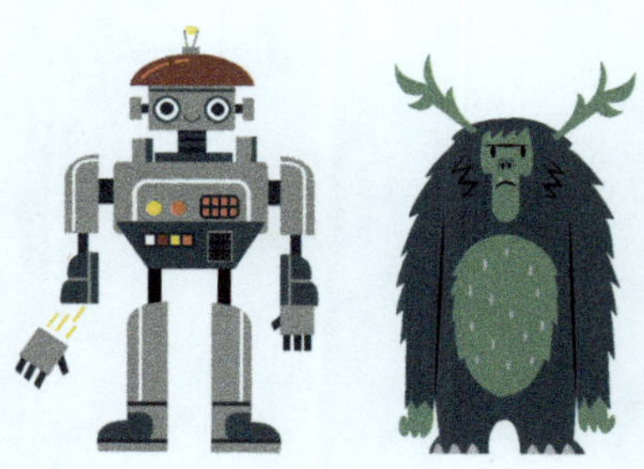

INTRODUCTION

A NEW SINCERITY

Hello, and thank you for buying this book.

To introduce myself, I want to tell you two specific things about me.

1. Since I was five years old, I have loved robots and monsters. Absolutely loved them. Still do. I can't fully explain why, but I can tell you that love comes from a deep, special place in me. Some of the most creative and interesting things I've ever done have come from that same place.

2. Since I was thirteen, I've had forty-seven different jobs.

Well, forty-eight if you count "author."

According to the U.S. Bureau of Labor Statistics, the average number of jobs most people will have in their lifetime is about twelve and a half. So if you're reading this, you probably land somewhere around ten to fifteen.

I've been fired from more jobs than some people have had, period.

I'm not here to recommend collecting jobs like Pokémon cards. However, I can tell you it gave me a unique perspective. Looking back, I can see that my career moved through a few distinct eras, and reflecting on those eras revealed something surprising:

Some of the strategies I learned are useful to anyone, in any profession, in any season of life.

Throughout my work history, the creativity in me that began with that deep love for robots and monsters has been my most valuable asset. It helped me pick myself up after a fall. It helped me find the next adventure. It helped me do meaningful work, even when the circumstances were not ideal.

So we're going to frame this book around three creative eras in the Hero's Journey: Dream Bigger, Inner Compass, and Mad Skills. If you're unfamiliar, on the Hero's Journey, the hero leaves home, faces trials, discovers allies, defeats monsters, and finally returns with something valuable.

I'll tell you about the jobs I've had and the lessons I learned the hard way. I'll share strategies you can test and adapt to your own life. And I'll offer exercises because creativity is something you practice.

Your career won't have the same eras as mine does.

It probably won't have the same strategies.

Maybe robots and monsters aren't your thing.

But I believe you'll find something here that clicks. A sentence that unlocks a memory. A tool that gets you moving again. A way of thinking that helps you thrive in whatever creative era you're in now.

This book is not really about my career.

It's about yours.

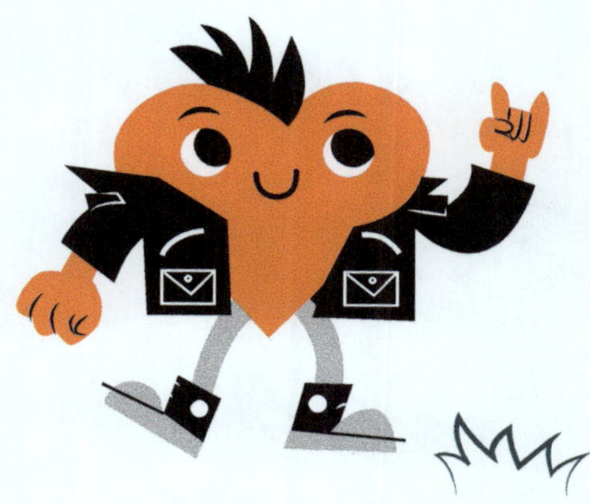

THE PHILOSOPHY OF CARING AS REBELLION

Somewhere in my life, a switch was thrown.

I can't remember the exact moment it flipped, but accepting it felt as profound as leaving childhood behind and stepping clearly into adulthood.

My love for robots and monsters started early. I was a latchkey kid with two working parents, and TV was often my babysitter. *Looney Tunes* was the discipline of the day.

One cartoon in particular still lives in my brain: "Hair-Raising Hare" (1946), starring Bugs Bunny and the orange-haired monster, Gossamer. To this day, it might still be the funniest cartoon I've ever seen.

I loved Bugs. I admired his wit, quick thinking, spontaneity, and sarcasm. Bugs never acted until he was provoked, pushed to the wall, and then he responded with a kiss on the lips, a pie to the face, and a remark sharp enough to cut glass. He wasn't the biggest or the strongest. He was the smartest.

Somewhere along the way, that became my personality.

Not the kiss and the pie. I'm not a monster.

I started to associate quickness, being fast with a comeback, as intelligence. For this kid who struggled every day in school from kindergarten to high school, it was a solution to almost everything. It played well with my ADHD brain because I could think fast on my feet and run circles around most people. It felt like a superpower.

It also worked as a shield.

Sarcasm, irony, and cynicism gave me distance. They kept people and feelings at bay. If I was flippant enough, then I was in control. If I didn't care, I couldn't be hurt. If I laughed first, no one could laugh at me. For a sensitive kid who felt like an open nerve, that mattered.

Childhood, in many ways, is survival. You collect skills to get through whatever life hands you. Some of those skills are beautiful. Some are defensive.

For a while, my armor worked. Or I thought it did.

Armor always has a cost. Over time, it gets heavy. It rubs you raw. Eventually, it stops doing what you built it to do.

As I matured, I began to notice the subtle ways it was failing me.

I could wave away missed goals with a shrug.

I could deflect hard conversations with a joke.

I started to lose friends and alienate family members who didn't want to keep bouncing off my walls.

Worst of all, I wasn't showing up honestly in my own life, and I knew it.

For an artist, that's a problem. If we can't access our feelings, real thoughts, and our actual tenderness, then what exactly are we making? What do we offer?

At some point, the persona starts to feel like a performance. Somewhere around age thirty, it hit me that the life I was headed toward wasn't one I wanted.

I didn't want to be "untouchable."

I wanted to be connected.

I wanted integrity.

I wanted a life with family, kids, dear friends, and a creative path I could walk without faking it.

So I did the thing my armor was designed to prevent and looked in the mirror.

I started paying attention to the people I truly admired. Not the loudest or coolest. Not the ones with the slickest "brand." The ones who seemed fully alive.

Then I noticed a trait they shared, earnestness. Guilelessness, an open-hearted devotion to the things they loved. They weren't performing detachment or trying to be above it all. If they cared about something, even if it was obscure, uncool, or out of fashion, they cared openly. They pursued it. They protected it. They didn't apologize for it.

When I saw that, I had to admit something uncomfortable: I was scared.

Scared my true self wasn't lovable.

Scared the things I cared about could be used against me.

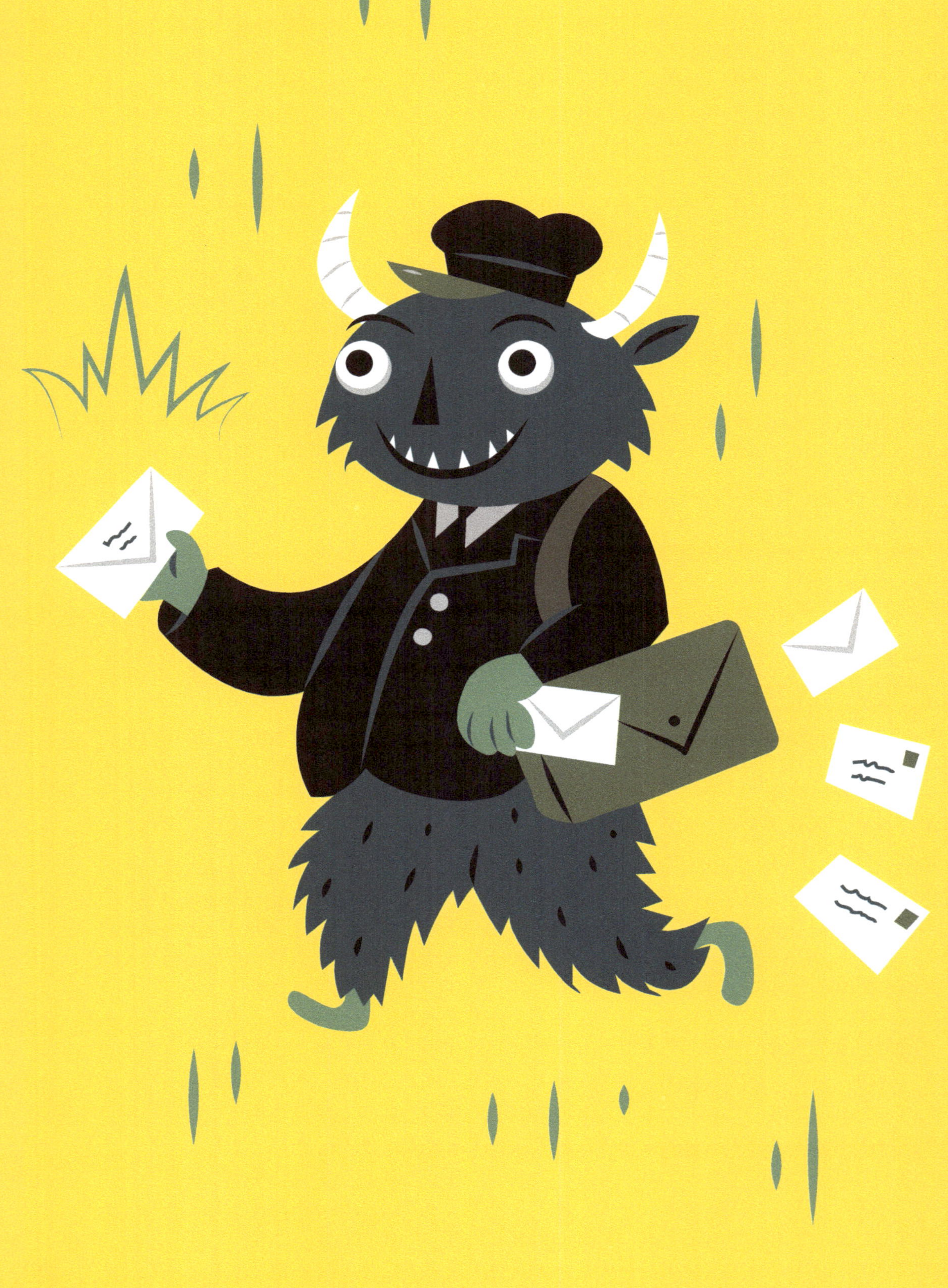

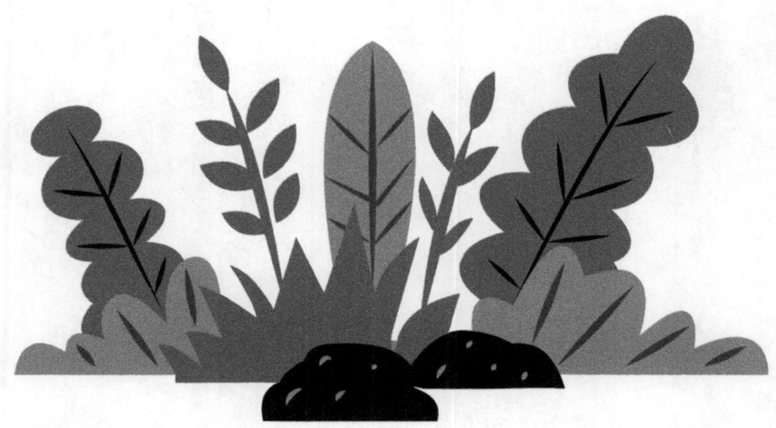

Scared that if I tried and failed, it would prove the cynical voice right.

Here's where the switch flipped and turned on the idea that caring was worth the risk.

I began to practice sincerity and vulnerability as courageous first steps. I didn't become humorless (I still love sarcasm), but I tried to aim it mostly at myself instead of using it as a weapon or a moat. I listen more than I talk. I show love toward the things I'm deeply into. I let myself be visibly moved by stories, art, music, ideas, sometimes to an embarrassing degree. In the end, I may have turned out less like Bugs and more like the misunderstood monster, Gossamer.

My vulnerability can confuse people. It can read as too much. Cringe.

But I'm done living from the cheap seats, heckling my own life. That's part of why I wrote this book. Creativity isn't just making art. It's taking a stance. It's a way to resist the deadening gravity of cynicism. It's refusing to let the world's exhaustion turn you into someone who can't feel.

In a bleak world, caring is rebellion.

So let's get into the strategies—practical, weird, and hard-won—for staying open-hearted long enough to make something that matters.

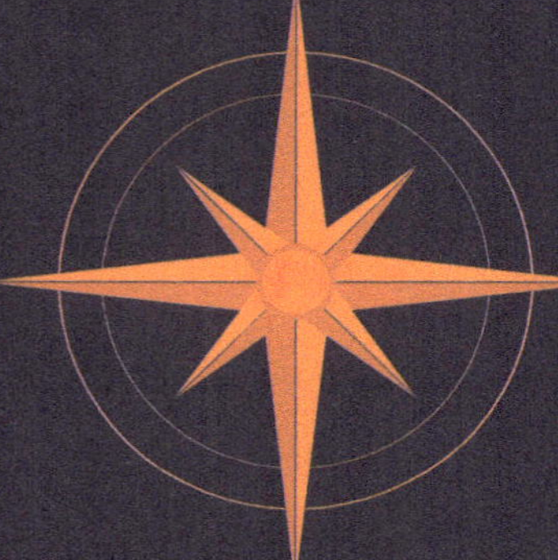
A NEW
SINCERITY
MAD
SKILLS
DREAM
BIGGER
INNER
COMPASS

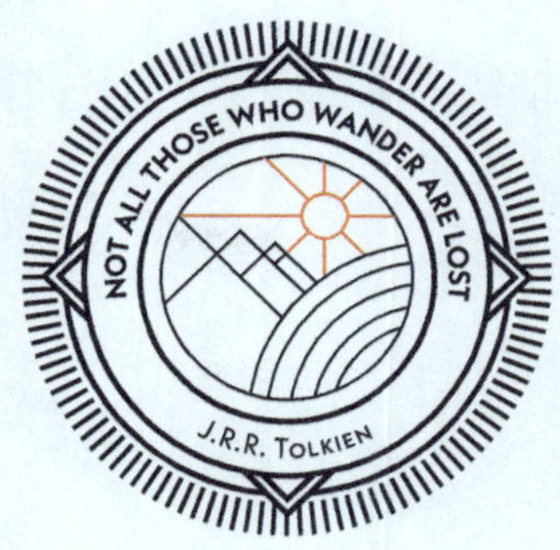

HOW TO USE THIS GUIDE

THE MAP AND COMPASS

Creativity is not a straight path. It's not even a single path.

Creativity flows more like a landscape, sometimes wide open, sometimes dense with trees, sometimes so foggy you can't see the next step. In every creative era of your life, you're navigating that terrain. Sometimes you have a map. Sometimes you have a compass. And sometimes, you feel like you have neither.

I've been creating for as long as I can remember, films, books, magazines, scripts, comics, and children's stories. For more than twenty years, I've led creative teams for startups and brands like Facebook™, Cisco®, Salesforce™, and ServiceNow®, and worked at creative powerhouses like Pixar® Animation Studios and Duarte Design. I've thrived in small startups and massive global organizations, and I've seen firsthand that creativity is a practice, mindset, and, at times, a fight.

In this book, we'll talk about sincerity, weirdness, mentors, monsters, and how to keep going when the trail gets rough.

Along the way, you'll find workshop-style exercises, invitations to stop reading and start doing. They're designed to help you explore your own creative process, uncover your unique voice, and build creative habits that last.

Whether you're in a period of explosive growth, a time of reevaluation, or deep mastery of your craft, this guide will help you thrive in any creative era.

WHAT CREATIVE ERA ARE YOU IN?

Circle the description that fits you best

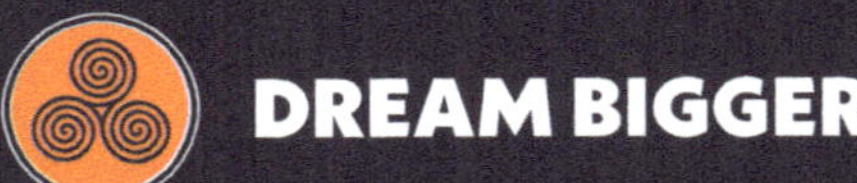 **DREAM BIGGER**

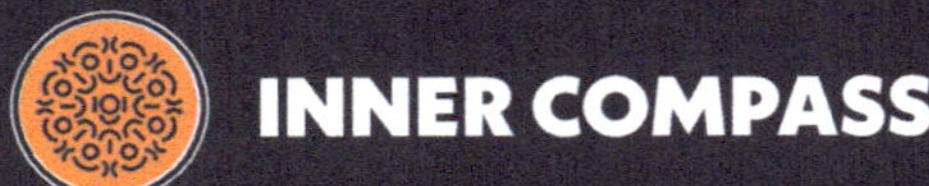 **INNER COMPASS**

I want to grow, stretch, and dream boldly.

You're ready to try something bold.

You want to build a future that lights you up.

You feel the pull of something new (even if it scares you).

I want to pause and reconnect with what feels real.

You're pivoting or re-evaluating what matters.

You've experienced some creative burnout.

You want more meaning in your work or art.

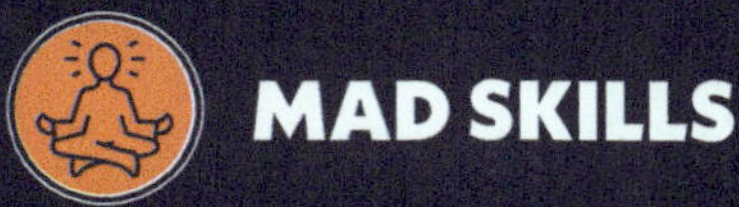

MAD SKILLS

I want to build, share, teach, or evolve my work.

You've honed your craft and want to go deeper.

You want to share, lead, or build legacy work.

You're ready to collaborate or teach.

DON'T WORRY YOU MIGHT BE A MIX.

The point is: you are in motion.

You might live in one era for years…or shift every few months. Knowing where you are helps you choose the right tools and pace.

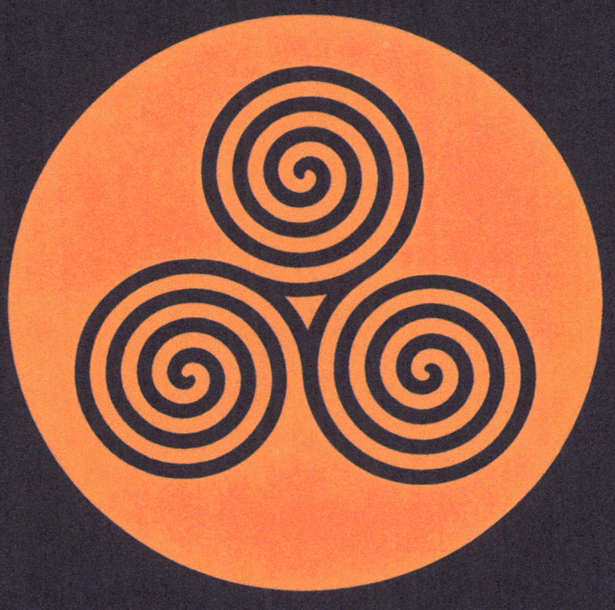

DREAM BIGGER

You've heard the call to adventure, and you can't ignore it anymore. Step out of the familiar and start moving toward the life you want. In this section, you'll follow the prize inside, find a mentor, and make a map you can actually use.

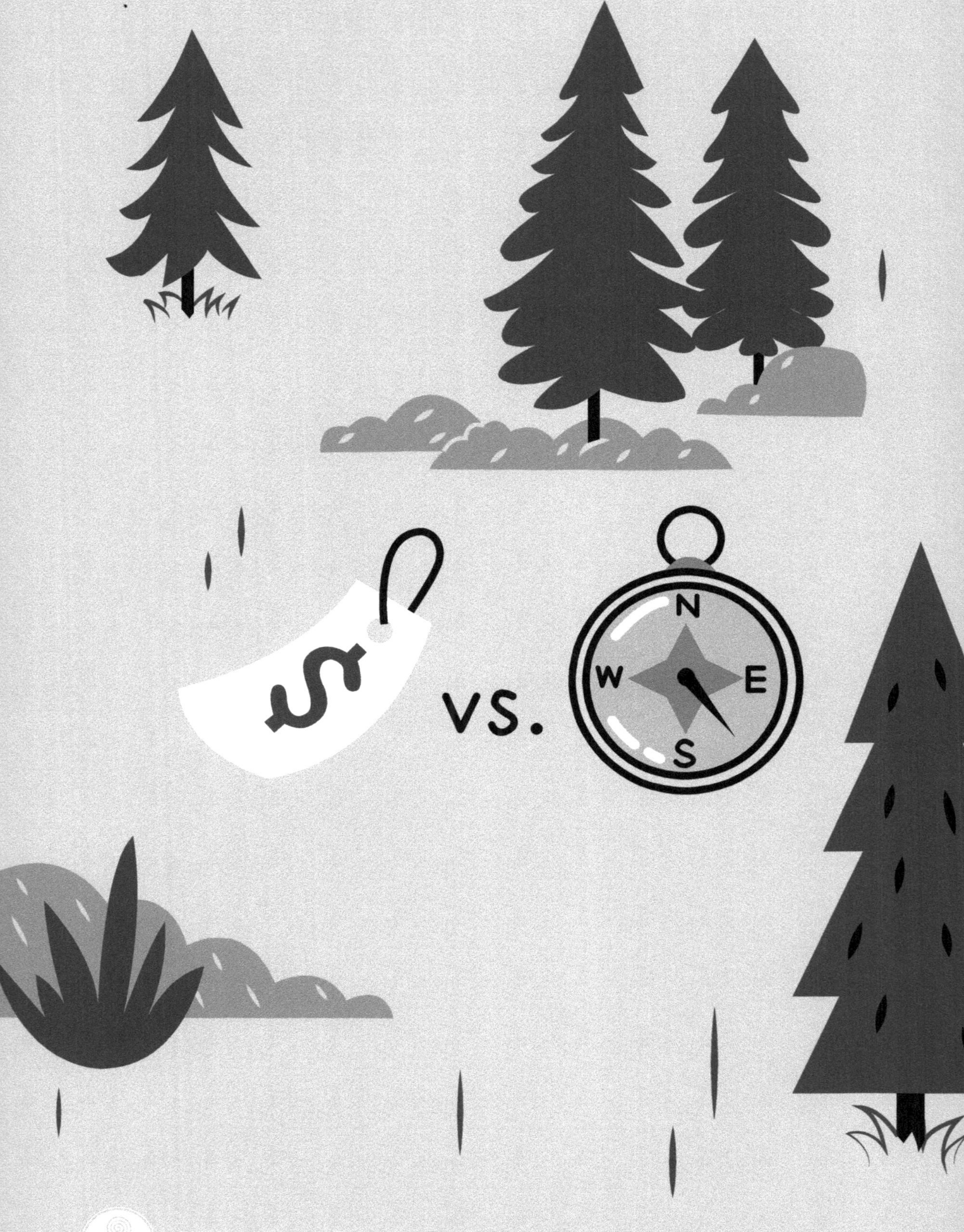

$
VS.
N
W
E
S
DREAM BIGGER

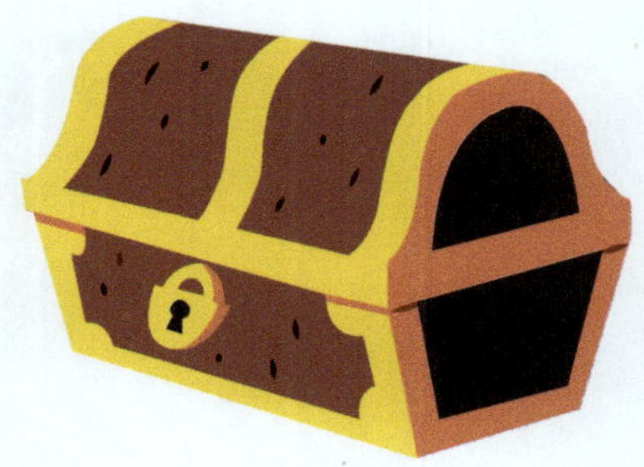

CHAPTER 01

THE PRIZE INSIDE: WHY JOY IS YOUR COMPASS

My forties started with a spectacular fall, though I didn't think so at the time.

I was working at a job that I just LOVED. I enjoyed the work, got to travel frequently, and the people were great. I was really happy. One of the best jobs I've ever had.

While I was working there, I got recruited. Have you ever been recruited by someone? Wow, that can be intoxicating. This guy took me to a nice restaurant for dinner, wined and dined me, asked me to come work at his company, and offered me a decent salary bump. It sounded really good.

Good enough for me to make the change.

Within weeks of starting my new role as creative director, I poured myself into my first big idea. It was a brand mascot, a robot with a backstory and endless potential. I could see a hundred ways it would work with ads, comics, conference booths, stickers, and a whole universe of brand expression. I was on fire.

I pitched it with everything I had.

They hated it.

They didn't see it. Didn't like it. Didn't want it. However you want to say it, my robot didn't fly.

And that wasn't the first of my ideas that didn't fly. It became clear that this company wasn't interested in an infusion of creativity. I was pretty bummed that I had left a job that I enjoyed for a place that didn't appreciate what I had to offer.

Then I got laid off.

That moment stung because I had traded joy for prestige, and the price was steep.

Looking back, I see the gift inside that gut punch: Joy is the compass.

SATURDAY MORNING MAGIC

Let's rewind a bit. Raise your hand if you grew up watching Saturday morning cartoons. The real deal of waking up way too early, a giant bowl of sugary cereal, and your legs going numb on the carpet.

That was pure magic for me. Robots and monsters. Heroes flattened by anvils only to bounce back with a grin. A bottomless bowl of Technicolor joy.

Those Saturday mornings were a great source of joy for me. Infinite wonder and possibility and happiness. I've been chasing that feeling my whole career.

Tapping into wonder and possibility is one of the most important tools we have as creatives, our ability to recognize and seek that source of joy in ourselves. And that joy often impacts our career, too.

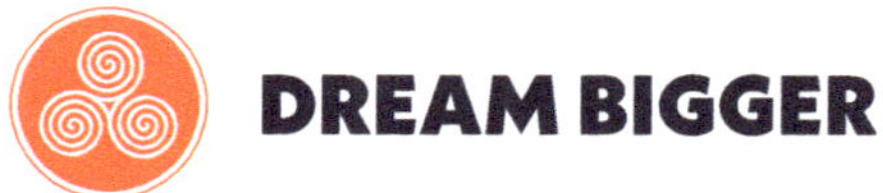

When we lose track of that spark of joy, cynicism creeps in dressed as fear in a leather jacket. Fear of caring too much. Fear of being wrong. Fear of looking silly. It makes you feel smart and safe, but really, it's joy's worst enemy.

That day, my robot pitch died? That was cynicism moving in, and I let it rob me of joy.

Cynicism kills joy. Every time.

THE PRIZE INSIDE

Remember cereal boxes that came with a prize inside? Decoder rings, tiny toy cars, goofy trinkets that made your morning feel epic. That's how I think about joy.

Joy is the prize inside. In creative work, it's the clearest signal you're heading in the right direction. Joy fuels resilience and helps you bounce back after rejection or failure.

Following the spark is scary but essential because the things that light you up are fuel. We're here today, chasing that prize. We're pointing our compass toward joy, even when the map runs out.

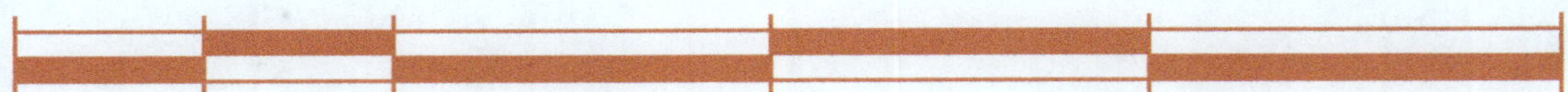

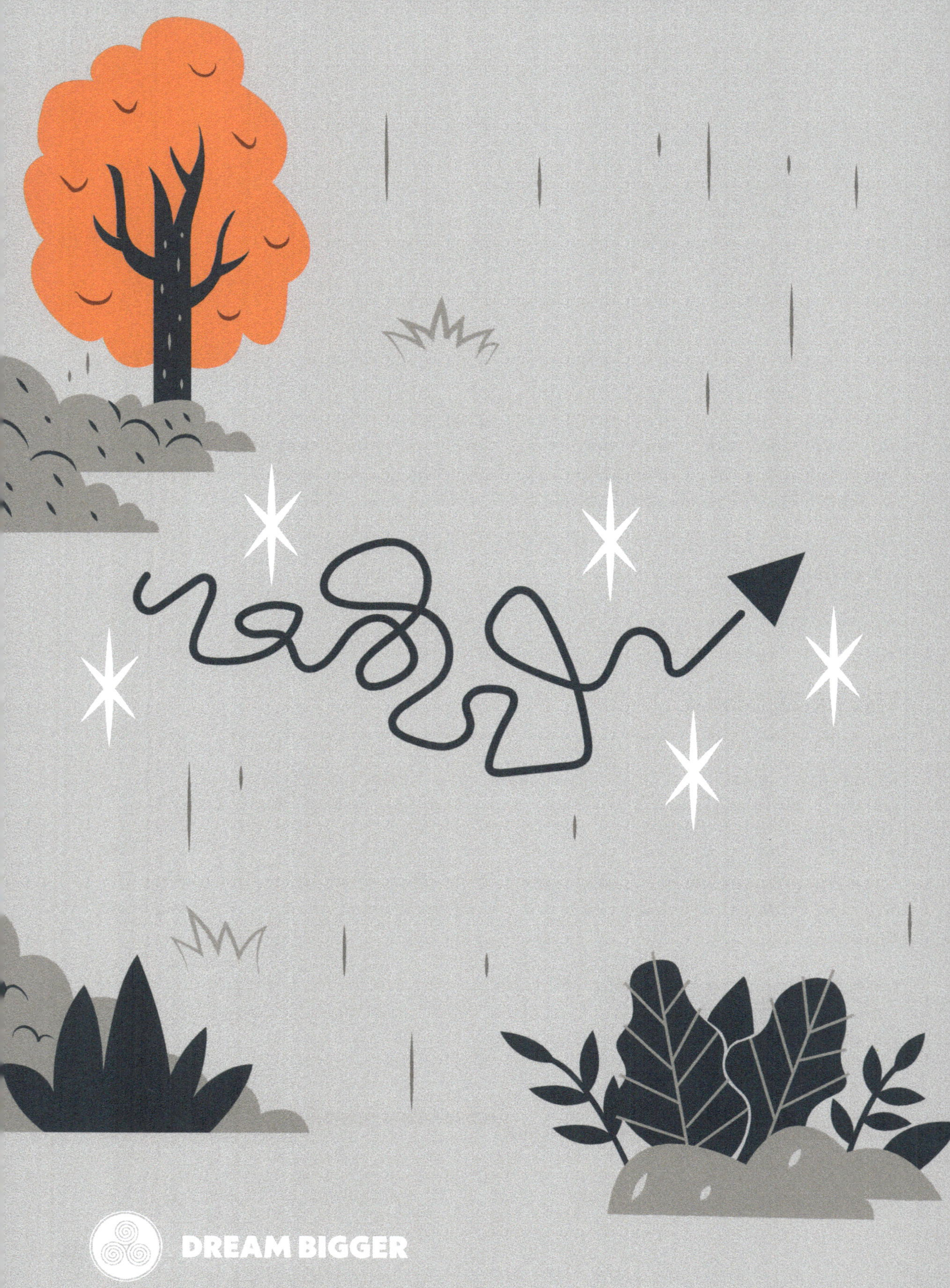
DREAM BIGGER

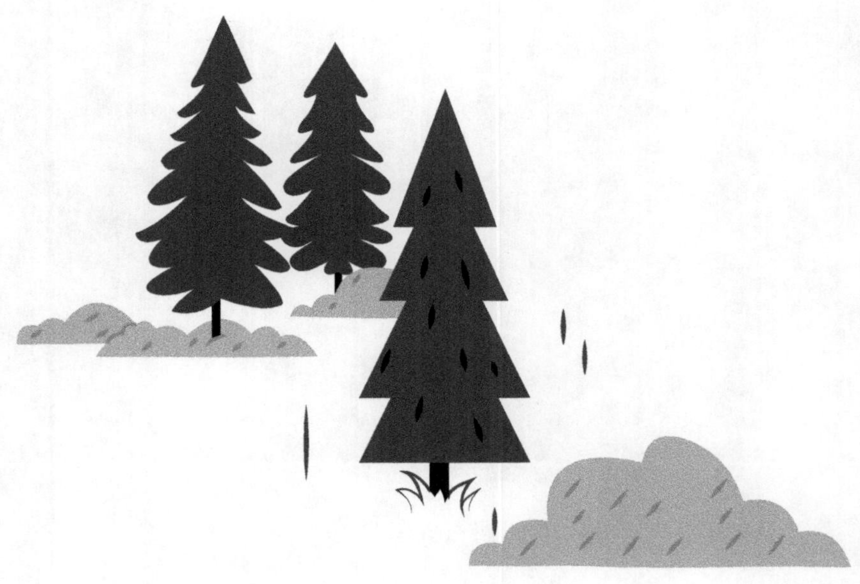

WHAT HAPPENED NEXT

A few years after the layoff, I found myself at Pixar®. On paper, that was the dream job, the holy grail for a kid who grew up obsessed with robots and monsters. In many ways, it was extraordinary with brilliant colleagues, world-class storytelling, and the magic of watching sketches come to life on screen.

Even there, the compass mattered. Pixar® Animation Studios wasn't exactly what I wanted. I had incredible experiences and met artists who still inspire me today, but after a couple of years, I wanted to go back to school and earn an MFA in illustration, with an eye on teaching someday.

Joy kept nudging me forward, pointing me toward other adventures and ways to use my weird skills. That's when I realized that joy isn't landing the perfect job. True joy is building a creative life that keeps you lit up.

INSIGHT

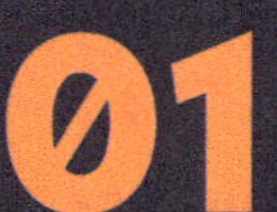
01
CYNICISM IS JUST FEAR IN DISGUISE. Sincerity takes more courage, but it unlocks creativity and connection.

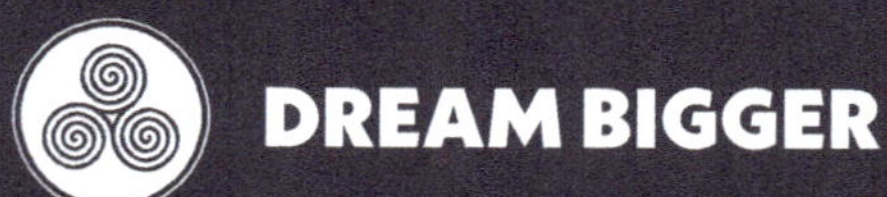
DREAM BIGGER

THE CYNICISM DETOX

Sincerity is your superpower. Cynicism feels safe, but it's really armor. It blocks wonder before it has a chance to land. This exercise helps you drop the armor and step back into curiosity.

1	**SPOT THE ARMOR**	Write down three situations, projects, or ideas where you've recently felt "too cool," "above it," or quick to roll your eyes.
2	**NAME THE FEAR**	For each, uncover the shadow underneath. What might you be afraid of? (Looking foolish? Wasting time? Being rejected?)
3	**FLIP IT**	Choose one. Do the thing you've been dismissing. Try it earnestly. Show up with curiosity instead of irony. Imagine your 10-year-old self cheering you on.
4	**REFLECT + REWARD**	At the end of the week, note how it felt. Did it open up new possibilities? Then, reward yourself (coffee, walk, music break) because sincerity is brave, and brave deserves celebration.

"
CYNICISM PROTECTS YOU FROM THE WORLD.

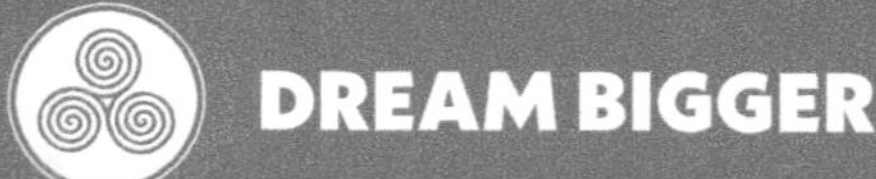
DREAM BIGGER

SINCERITY CONNECTS YOU TO IT.

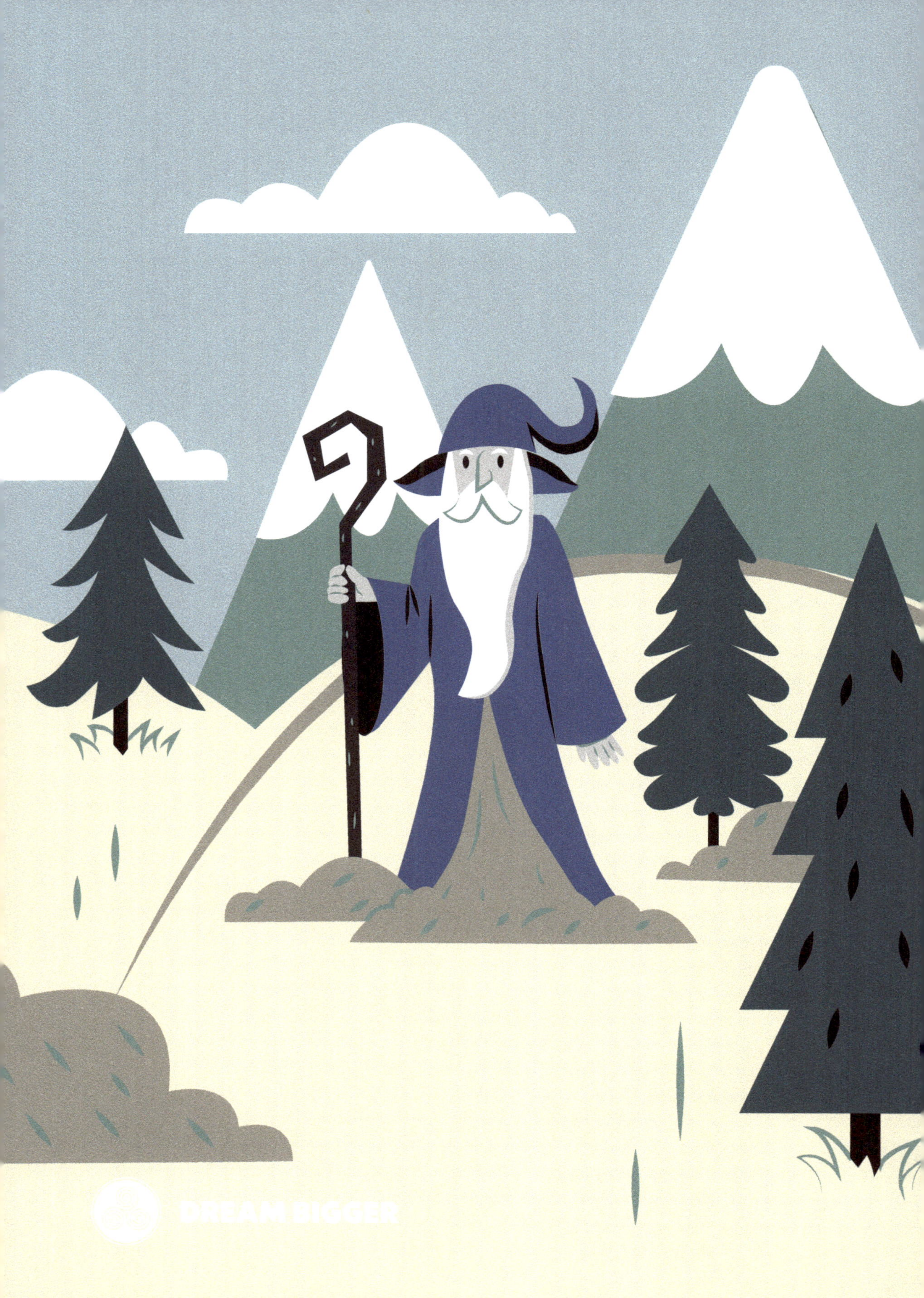
DREAM BIGGER

CHAPTER 02

MEET YOUR MENTOR: WHY YOU NEED A GUIDE

Another time, in my thirties, I had gotten what I thought was my dream job as art director at a gaming magazine. It was an awesome company in a world I genuinely loved. Great people. Fun work. A solid future, and I planned to be there for a long time.

Around the same time, I was dating a woman I loved. I felt like I'd finally made it and reached stable ground, so I decided that over the Christmas holiday, I would propose.

She said yes.

Then the holidays ended, and I went back to work at my dream job.

You can probably guess what happened next. Yep, they laid me off.

It wasn't the first time I'd lost a job, but it was the worst. The timing felt almost cruel. I had just gotten engaged, had just pictured my life becoming steady, and the rug got yanked out so hard I didn't even know which way was up.

I shattered.

Not long after that, I found myself on the couch. Jobless. Engaged, but ashamed. While my fiancée was planning our wedding, I could barely get up. It felt like I had climbed the ladder, done everything right, reached the checkpoint, and then fell straight to the bottom.

Ever been there?

I told myself I'd recover quickly. I'd hustle and figure it out. The truth was I was paralyzed.

Somewhere in that fog, a darker thought started circling. *Maybe my best work was already behind me.*

At the time, my fiancée was studying to become a certified life coach. I didn't even really understand what a life coach was, but she suggested I find one for myself.

I did. It was the best thing that came out of that crash.

Her name is Ginny. I hired her to be my life coach, which is a fancy way of saying that you work with someone trained to hold space, ask sharp questions, listen without flinching, and help you find your next steps.

Session by session, I started to come back. But the biggest gift she gave me was scale.

When I was stuck staring at the wreckage, she helped lift my eyes. She helped me think bigger than the job title. Bigger than the ladder. Bigger than the version of success I'd been chasing like it was the only door out.

That's what a real mentor does.

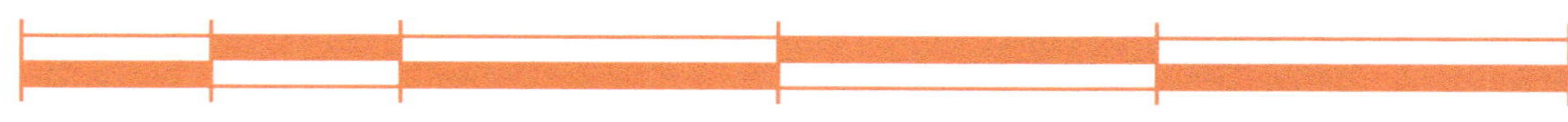

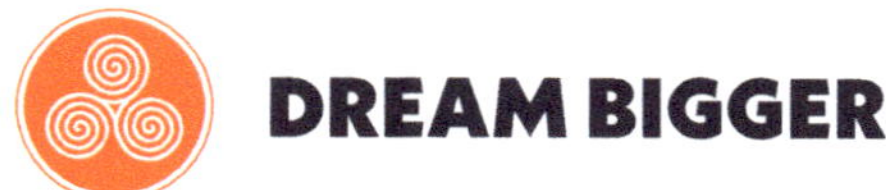

THE QUESTION THAT CHANGED EVERYTHING

In our first session, Ginny didn't ask about my résumé or for a list of goals. She looked at me and asked, "What were you obsessed with before the world told you to be realistic?"

That question stopped me cold.

Then I started rambling about robots and cereal box prizes. About the monsters I used to doodle in the margins of math homework. About comic books stacked in my childhood room.

Her face lit up. "That's the treasure," she said. "That's the thread. Pull it."

Just like that, the fog began to lift. The question wasn't really about hobbies. It was about my identity, the parts of me that existed before fear, status, and performance. The parts of me that made things just because I loved making them.

WHY IT MATTERS

Every creative career is too big to navigate alone.

At some point, we all need a guide, someone who sees what we can't see, who holds steady when we've lost our footing, who reminds us of the treasure we already carry.

For me, that was Ginny.

For you, it might be a teacher, colleague, neighbor, coach, or friend with a talent you admire, or a creative elder who tells you the truth with kindness.

BENEFITS OF WORKING WITH A COACH

Coaching can help you set and achieve the goals that are most important to you.

Get clarity on priorities and values.

When you're pulled in a dozen directions, a mentor helps you sort what truly matters from the noise.

Set short-term, mid-term, long-term goals

Big dreams need a ladder. A mentor helps you map the rungs in a way that feels achievable.

Create action plan with tangible steps.

Not vague intentions, but specific moves you can take this week, this month, this year.

HOW TO WORK WITH A MENTOR

BE BRAVE.
Don't stay comfortable. Take risks and move forward.

DO THE WORK.
Read, write, practice. Follow through on their guidance.

BE HONEST.
Bring your whole truth. They can't help with what you hide.

BE ON TIME.
Respect the relationship. The way you'd respect your career.

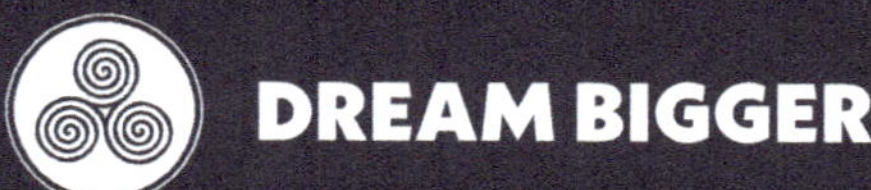

Stay motivated through the lows.

Creative block, self-doubt, or life stress? A mentor helps you reframe, recharge, and keep moving forward.

Navigate the business side of creativity.

Contracts, pricing, marketing yourself, the unglamorous stuff that makes your art sustainable.

REMEMBER, MENTORS AREN'T ALWAYS FOREVER.

Sometimes they're there for one season, and a season can change your whole life.

WEIRD-O WISDOM

Think of three people who influenced your life, work, or creativity. They do not need to be formal mentors. In fact, better if they are gloriously odd.

1	**WHO WERE THEY?**	A boss, teacher, friend, coach, relative, artist, neighbor, or passing guide.
2	**WHAT MADE THEM A WEIRD-O?**	What was their odd obsession, quirky habit, strange style, unforgettable energy, or very specific flavor of humanity?
3	**WHAT DID THEY TEACH YOU?**	A skill, a value, a way of seeing, a way of leading, a way of surviving.
4	**WHAT PART OF THAT LIVES IN YOU NOW?**	What did you absorb, borrow, or become because of them?

WHAT KIND OF WEIRD-O ARE YOU BECOMING FOR SOMEONE ELSE?

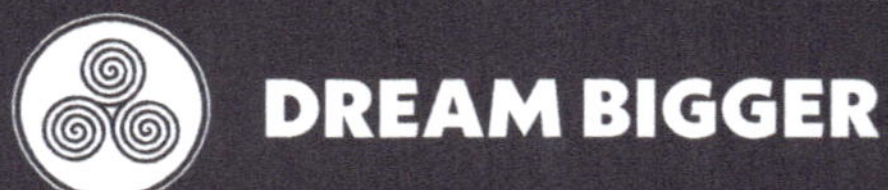

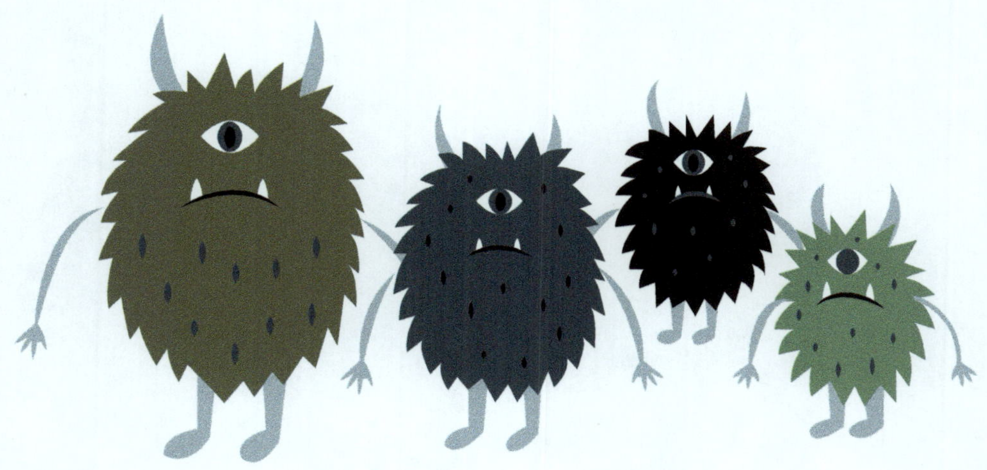

MENTORS, GUIDES, AND GLORIOUS WEIRD-OS

Sometimes, to truly thrive, the bravest thing you can do is admit you're lost and let someone walk beside you until you find your compass again. Once you start paying attention, you realize mentors come in all shapes and sizes. The only real requirement is that you have to be open enough to recognize them when they arrive.

Sometimes they show up older and wiser, exactly as advertised. Sometimes, annoyingly, they show up younger than you, carrying a skill you haven't unlocked yet.

That was the case with my friend Jonah.

Jonah arrived when I was being hired into senior roles. My résumé looked legit, but if I'm honest, my creative chops didn't fully match the paper version of me yet.

Jonah leveled me up.

Where I had a strong right-brained instinct for story, feeling, punch, and vibe, Jonah brought structure, systems, and craft discipline. A calm, surgical way of making design decisions. He not only improved my work; he rewired how I thought about my work.

After a year or two alongside him, my confidence grew because my skills finally started catching up to my résumé.

Jonah is also a true weird-o in the best sense of the word, obsessed with vintage Schwinn Sting-Ray bikes from the sixties and seventies, classic video games, mid-century modern design, and vintage cars. Brother from another mother.

I'm grateful my pride didn't get in the way, because the moment you decide you're "too senior" to learn from someone is the moment your growth stops.

I've also been blessed with mentors who shaped me before I even understood what was happening.

There was Emma, a London-born, motorcycle-riding art director who had my back for the first time in my professional life. She had steely resolve in meetings and a firebrand backbone under the British stiff-upper-lip exterior. Emma taught me to protect our teammates. Support them even when they make mistakes. As a leader, you take the heat for the people under you.

Then there was Frederique, a Parisian creative director at one of the first startups I worked at, who lived on a houseboat in the San Francisco harbor. He felt like a character out of a Fellini film, effortless charm, unpredictable joy, and the sense that life was art and art was a reason to live. Frederique taught me that joy isn't

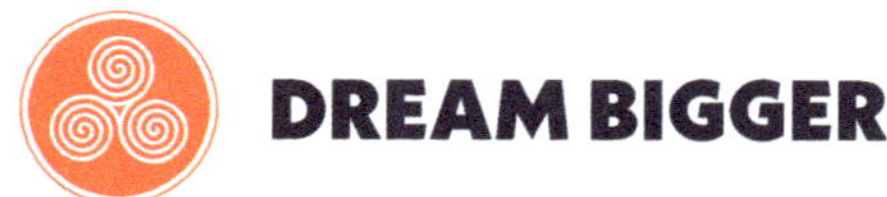

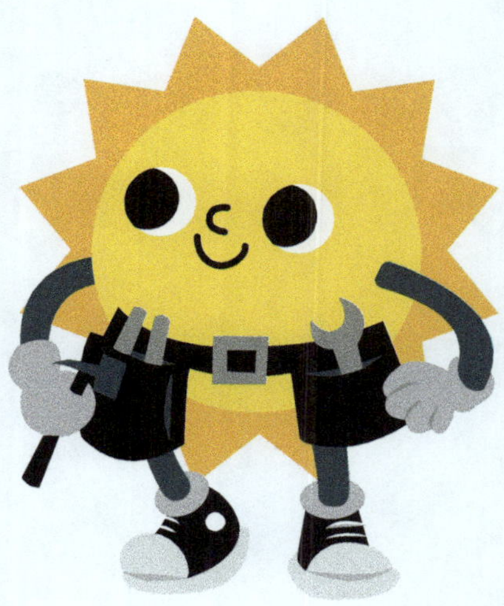

a "nice extra" at work. Joy is fuel that builds trust and binds teams. When a team feels human together, the work gets better.

And today, there is Nico, a painter from Los Angeles. Open-hearted and kind, and also tough when his back is against the wall. He tells stories from his grunge rock days in the early nineties of cutting his first record, touring, and living big. Later, he became a painter, opened galleries, and built a life that looked like momentum and magic…until it all came tumbling down.

That's where the mentorship got real.

Nico taught me about rediscovery. Starting again when you don't feel like you have anything left. Getting knocked down six times, getting up seven. Now he runs a successful nonprofit for kids. He teaches art, gives back, and builds community.

That's the strange thing about mentors. Sometimes they level up your skills. Sometimes they show you how to treat people. Sometimes they teach you how to rebuild from rubble.

But they always come into your life for a reason.

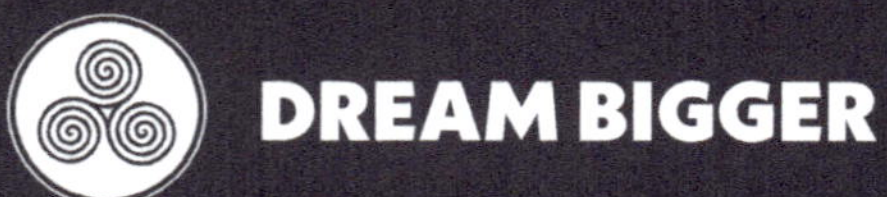
DREAM BIGGER

FIVE POTENTIAL GUIDES

Think about where you are in your creative era (Hero's Journey).
What kind of support do you need most right now? Clarity on your priorities and values?
Or simply someone to remind you of your strengths when you've forgotten them?

1	**LIST THREE**	People in your life who light you up creatively. Write down one trait or skill each has that you'd like to develop.
2	**ADD TWO LONG SHOTS**	People you admire but don't know personally, an industry leader, an artist you follow, a writer whose voice inspires you.
3	**FOR EACH NAME**	Note what kind of support you imagine they could provide (clarity, accountability, motivation, business guidance, etc.).
4	**CHOOSE ONE & REACH OUT**	Ask a question, share something you're working on, or simply invite them for coffee.

"

MENTORS DON'T ALWAYS ANNOUNCE THEIR ARRIVAL.

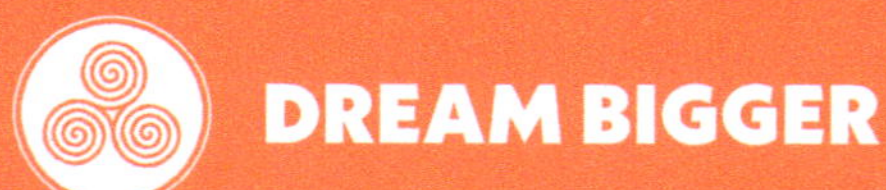

SOMETIMES THEY SHOW UP AS GLORIOUS WEIRDOS WHO CHANGE YOUR LIFE.

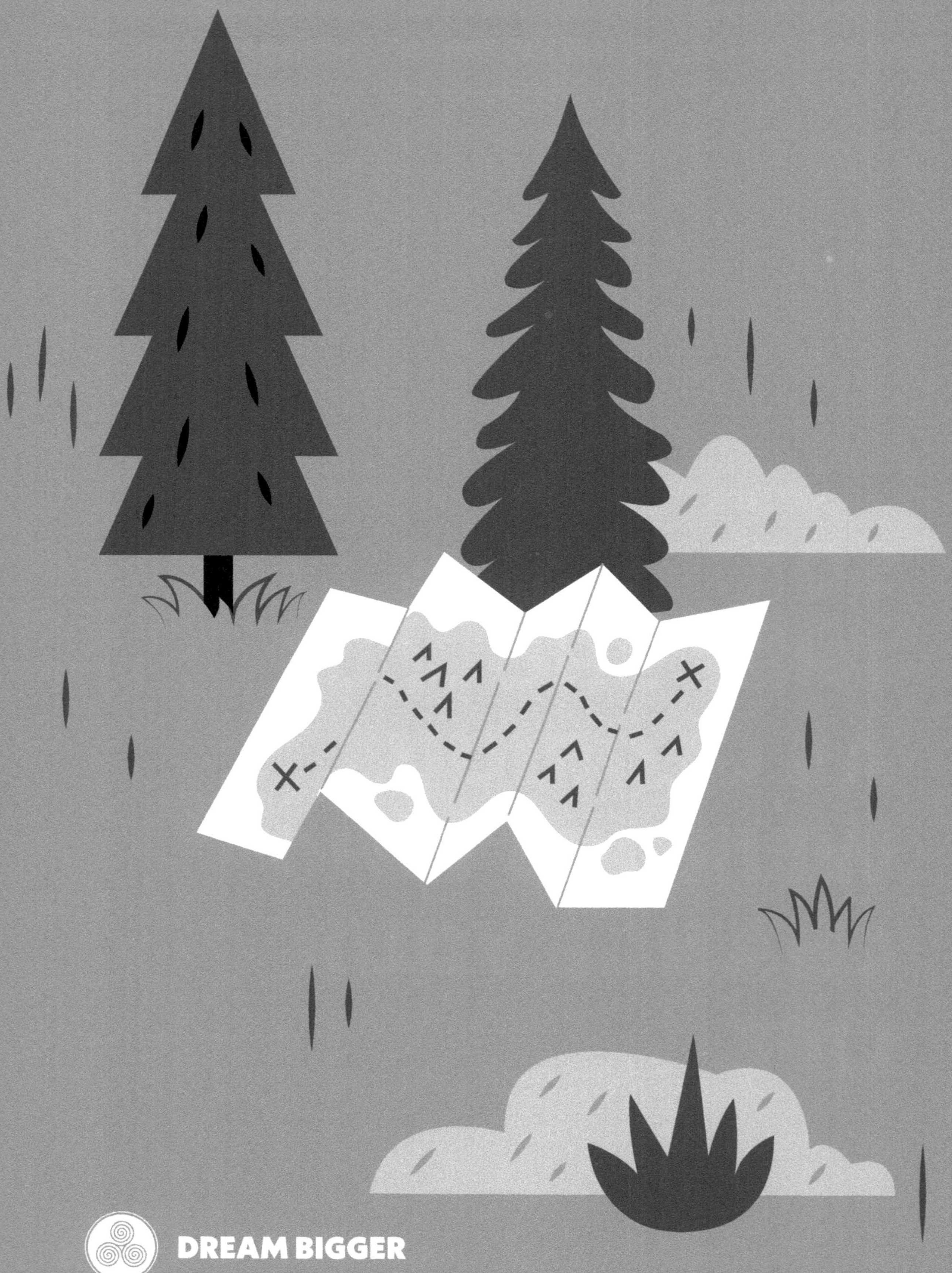

DREAM BIGGER

CHAPTER 03

A VISION BOARD IS A MAP: HOW TO CHART BIGGER DREAMS

Sometimes when you feel lost in life, you need a map. The kind that reminds you where you actually want to go when you're not performing, not panicking, not trying to sound impressive.

That's why I want to share a simple creative tool: the vision board.

A vision board is more than a craft project for people who collect inspirational quotes like baseball cards. It offers a personal compass, a way to chart bigger dreams when the path ahead feels foggy.

THE ASSIGNMENT I ALMOST LAUGHED AT

When Ginny first suggested I make a vision board, I almost rolled my eyes out of my head.

In my mind, vision boards belonged to cheesy self-help infomercials. Pictures of yachts, sports cars, and beach houses glued onto posterboard like a ransom note from your ego.

Ginny didn't blink. She pushed a pile of magazines across the table, handed me scissors and glue, and said, "Let's take this seriously."

So I did, and what I put on that board surprised me.

A picture of a cozy ranch-style house in the Bay Area, where housing prices were sky-high. It felt ridiculous to even want it.

Two twin beds for the kids I hoped to have someday. We had already been through years of infertility, so this one felt especially impossible.

The Pixar® logo. At the time, I was out of work and had no idea how I'd earn my way into that world.

All three felt so far out of reach they almost felt funny. Like I was auditioning for a life I didn't qualify for. But I stared at that board every day like it was a signal flare. A simple reminder of the direction I wanted my life to point. The board kept my compass pointed in the right direction long enough for my choices to start lining up.

Years later, I was living in that house. My wife and I had twins. I had a job at Pixar®.

WHY VISION BOARDS WORK

When you put your dreams somewhere you can actually see them, three things happen:

1. You remember what matters to you.

2. You filter opportunities through those priorities.

3. You notice connections you would have missed otherwise.

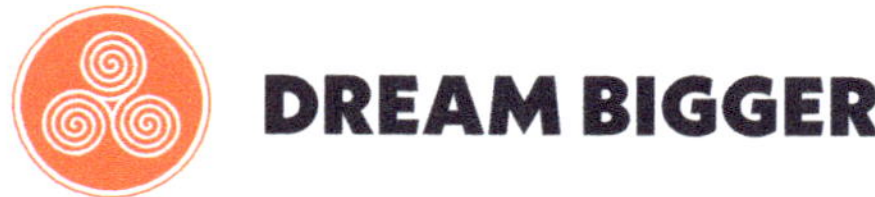

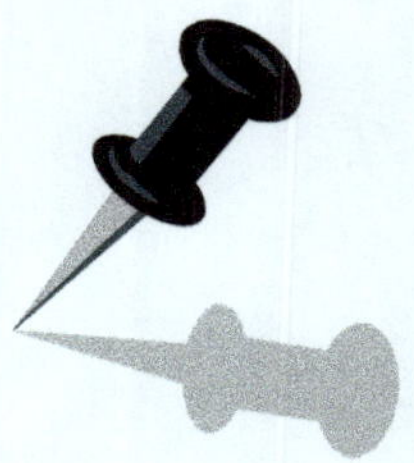

A vision board is less "I demand this exact future" and more "This is the direction I'm walking."

One thing I always add to my board is the phrase "This, or something better, for all involved."

This phrase keeps me open and humble. It keeps my vision from turning into a tight-fisted demand. Sometimes the exact thing shows up. Sometimes life delivers something even better than you couldn't have imagined when you were stuck on the couch, convinced your best days were behind you.

A MAP FOR BIGGER DREAMS

That first board wasn't really about a house, twins, or a dream job. It was about becoming the kind of person who could build that life. It was about giving myself permission to dream bigger than the disappointment I was sitting in.

You don't need a perfect map to move forward. It's time to create one that points you toward the kind of life you want to live.

Make it weird. Make it glittery. Make it yours.

Then let it guide you into your next adventure.

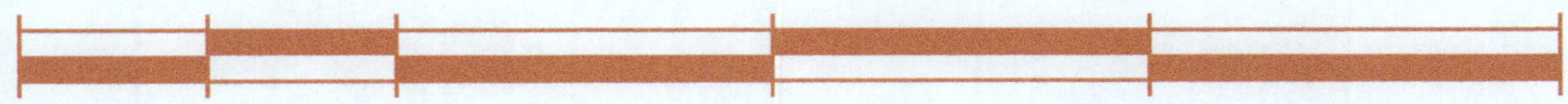

BUILD A VISION BOARD THAT ACTUALLY WORKS

You can do this with a posterboard and glue, or digitally with Canva, Pinterest, or Miro. Let's get started (and not judge the process).

Set your intention.

Ask: What do I want to call into my life?

Be specific enough to inspire action and open enough for surprise.

Collect what makes you feel something.

Images. Words. Colors. Symbols. Texture. Weird little things that spark you.

If it makes your chest feel warmer, keep it. Yes, use glitter if that's your thing.

Build the board like a story.

Don't overthink. Lay things out until it feels right.

If your board has chapters like health, home, relationships, and work, great. If it's a glorious chaotic collage, also great.

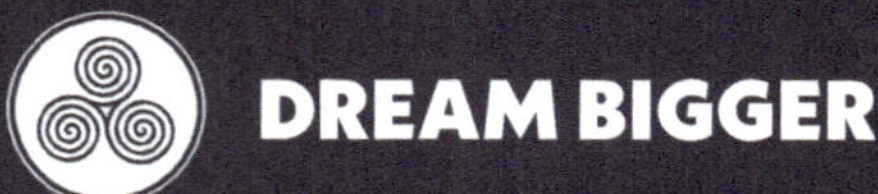

Add one honest picture of you.

Put it where you'll actually see it.

Not the LinkedIn headshot version of you. The real you. Radiant, alive, human.

Center it if you want. The goal isn't the stuff. It's who you're becoming.

Somewhere you'll bump into it often enough to remember, *This is where I'm headed.*

03

CLARITY ATTRACTS ACTION. When you can see your dreams, you can steer toward them.

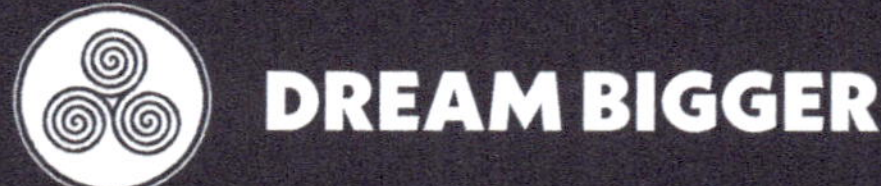

YOUR VISION MAP

It turns out, once you put it on the map, you'll be amazed how many roads start leading you there.

1	**CHOOSE YOUR TIMEFRAME**	Do you want to map the next 12 months? 5 years? A specific project?
2	**BRAINSTORM WITHOUT LIMITS**	Write down everything you want to experience, create, learn, or achieve. Try to align with your values not just material possessions you wish to aquire.
3	**FIND YOUR IMAGES & WORDS**	Gather visuals that light you up. Include power words, quotes, or even doodles.
4	**ASSEMBLE YOUR BOARD**	Arrange them in a way that feels right to you — clustered by theme, scattered by mood, or in a timeline.
5	**LIVE WITH IT**	Put it where you'll see it often. Let it remind you to choose in favor of your vision.

"
LIFE
PROVIDES
THE FOG.

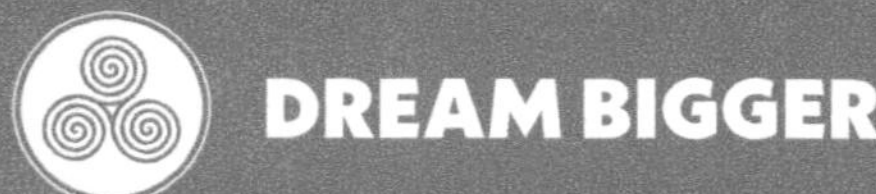
DREAM BIGGER

YOUR VISION BOARD PROVIDES THE STARS TO STEER BY.

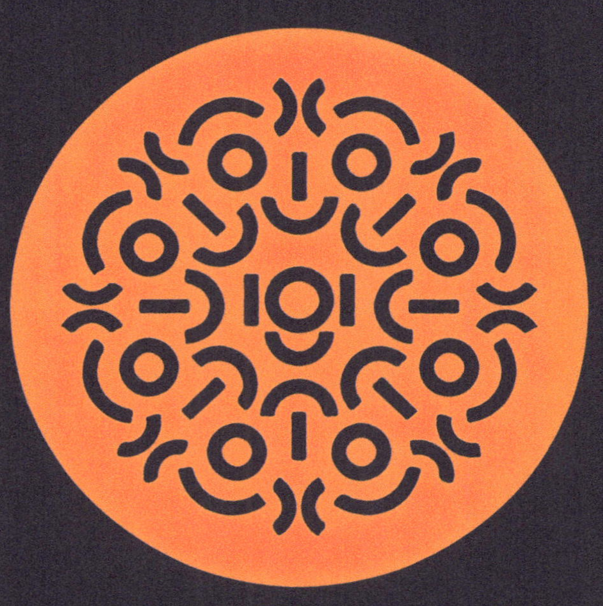

INNER COMPASS

You've started the Hero's Journey, but the road of trials is ahead, and this is where the real growth happens. Here's where the rubber meets the road: you'll outgrow your pond, battle monsters in disguise, and find your strength by unlocking the weird within.

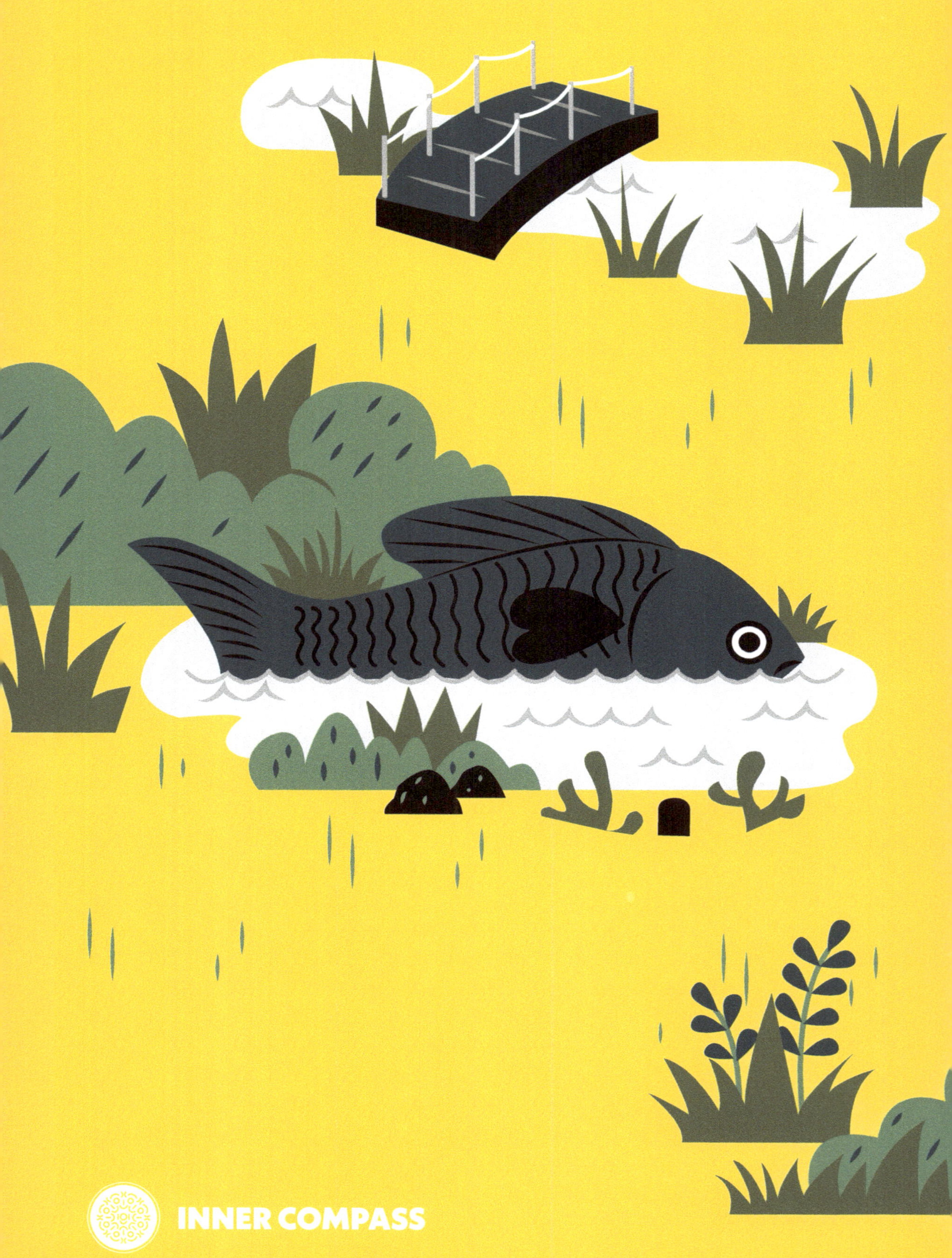
INNER COMPASS

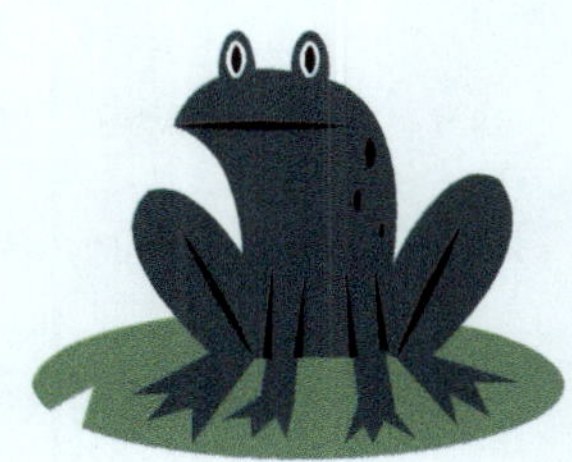

CHAPTER 04

THE FISH POND PRINCIPLE: FINDING THE RIGHT PLACE TO THRIVE

When I was younger, someone asked me, "Would you rather be a big fish in a small pond, or a small fish in a big pond?"

At the time, I thought the answer was obvious. Who wouldn't want to be the big fish? More recognition, more control, less competition. Easy.

The older I get, and the more jobs I work (forty-eight and counting), the more I realize that it's not that simple.

The real question isn't "Which is better?"

The real question is "Which pond will help you grow right now?"

CROSSING THE THRESHOLD: INTERNAL AND EXTERNAL

In stories, "crossing the threshold" is the heroic leap into the unknown. In real life, it often looks less like a leap and more like a fish outgrowing its pond.

Crossing the threshold usually happens in two parts:

The internal move. When you decide you're willing to be "small" again in exchange for a larger horizon.

The external move. You actually do it. Leave the comfortable job, switch industries, join the bigger team, and take the risk.

That internal decision matters because the big pond comes with a price
of humility.

You go from being confident and capable to being the new fish again, and
you've entered a bigger ecosystem.

MY POND-HOPPING YEARS

At Pixar®, I was a tiny fish in a vast ocean of talent. Walking into that building
was exhilarating and humbling. Geniuses working everywhere I turned, writers,
animators, designers. People so good they made me want to run faster just to
keep up.

Yes, it was intimidating and stretched me in ways nothing else could have.

At Duarte, I found myself in a different kind of pond. The company wasn't huge,
but the creative energy was massive. The design team was tight, scrappy, and
highly collaborative. Suddenly, I could experiment, take risks, and see my impact
immediately. That confidence became fuel.

Later, I joined a very large company with a very small design department.
Basically a puddle. And weirdly? That worked too. The scale of the company gave
me resources, but the size of the team gave me room to move to lead, shape
things, and make waves.

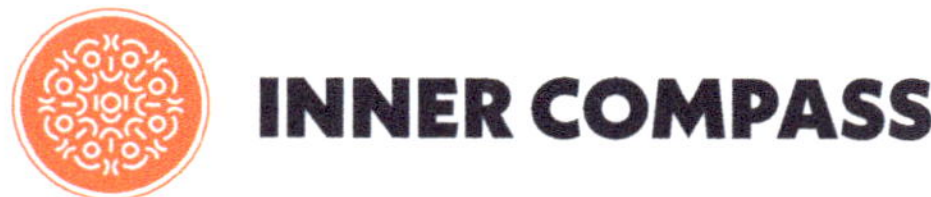

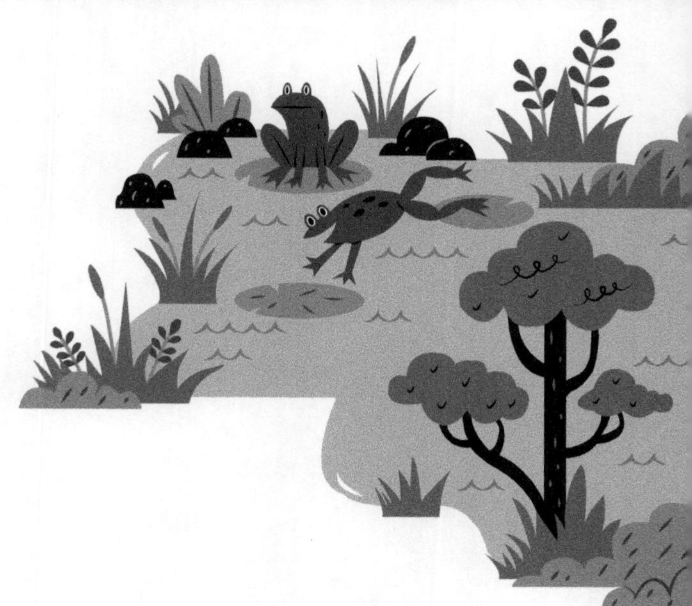

THE "JUST RIGHT" JOB

People sometimes call this the Goldilocks principle: too big, too small, just right.

I think that's true, but with one important twist: "Just right" doesn't mean "forever."

What's perfect today might be too small tomorrow. When that happens, it's a sign you grew.

SWIM ON

Looking back, I don't regret any of the ponds, even the puddles. Each one gave me something I needed at the time. IIs the same true for you?

Don't get stuck chasing the "perfect" pond.

Instead, find the water that gives you enough room to breathe and enough challenge to grow.

And when you outgrow it?

Swim on.

Thriving in your creative era is finding the water where you can come alive.

BIG FISH, SMALL POND

Small ponds can feel good. You know the terrain. You've mastered the environment. People recognize your strengths. You're trusted.

Range

You get to do a little of everything.

Confidence

Your impact is obvious.

Speed

You can try things without endless approval chains.

SMALL PONDS CAN ALSO CAUSE STAGNATION.

When you've mastered every corner of the pond, growth slows. Comfort can become a ceiling, and the real threat is staying too long.

Small ponds are great when you need range, confidence, and room to try things without the world watching.

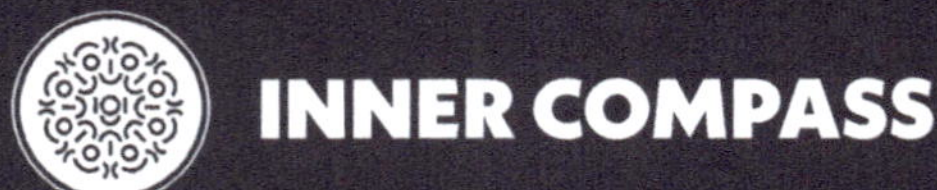

SMALL FISH, BIG POND

The big pond offers the opposite experience. The water is deeper. The creatures are bigger. The standards are higher.

Exposure

You're surrounded by mastery.

Challenge

You have to level up to survive.

Perspective

You see how the whole ecosystem works.

BIG PONDS MIGHT MAKE YOU FEEL INVISIBLE FOR A WHILE.

While it doesn't feel fun, that's the entry fee and won't last forever.

Big ponds are great when you need challenge, exposure, and a larger horizon to grow.

THE TRUTH ABOUT PONDS

There's no "right" pond forever. There's just the pond that fits your current season. Neither is better. They're just different kinds of growth.

04

LIKE A FISH, YOU GROW TO THE SIZE OF YOUR ENVIRONMENT.

The right "pond" shapes your creative growth.

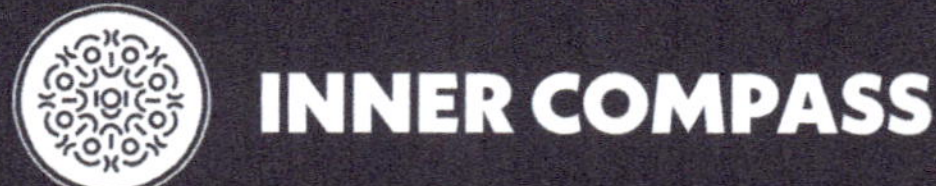

“
MOVING FROM A BIG FISH IN A SMALL POND TO A SMALL FISH IN A BIG POND

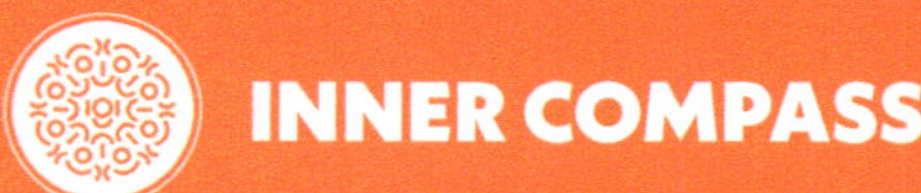

IS OFTEN THE HARDEST AND MOST REWARDING PIVOT YOU CAN MAKE.

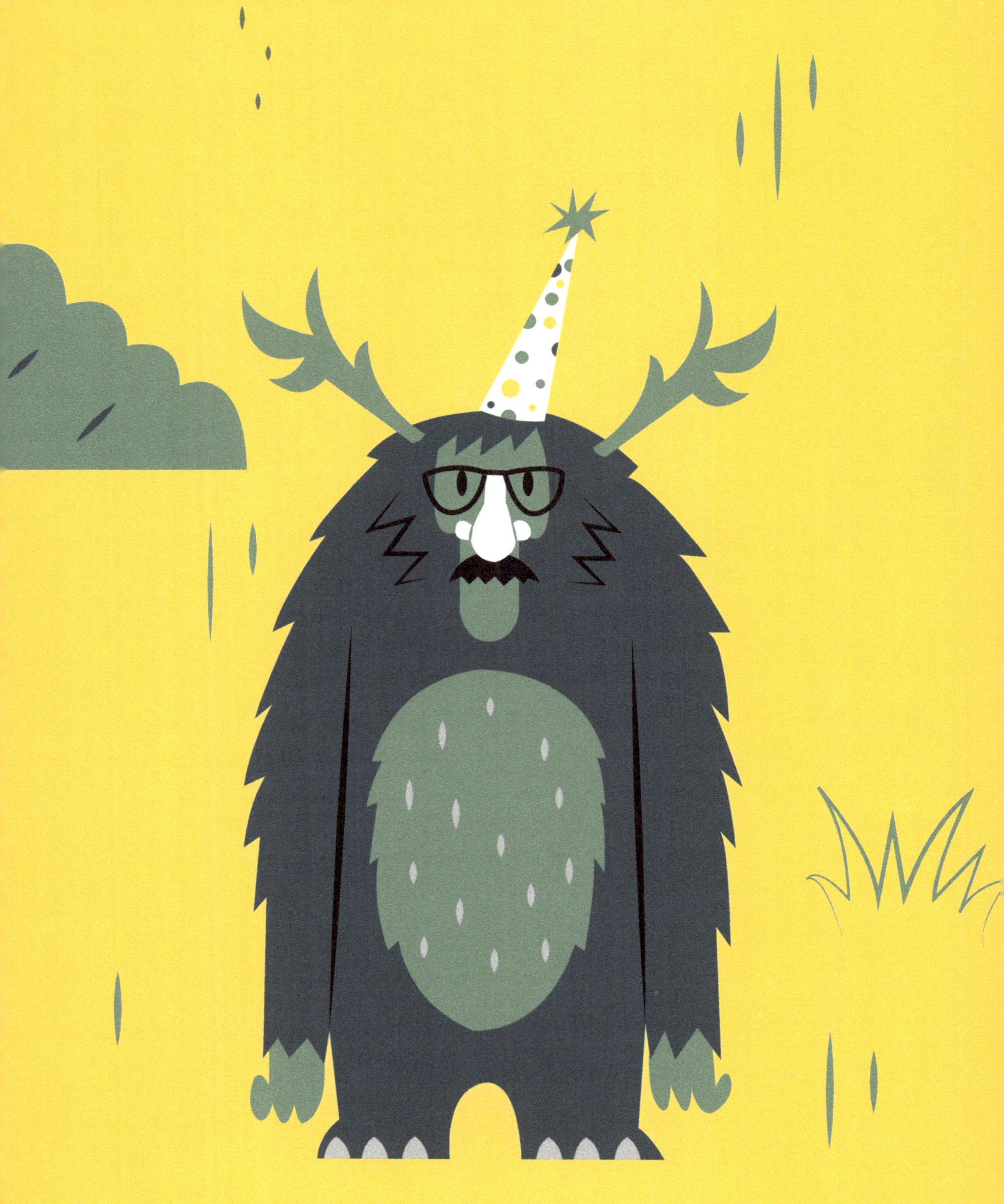

INNER COMPASS

CHAPTER 05

MONSTERS IN DISGUISE

Defeating the "monster" is rarely a physical battle. Most times, it's a psychological or spiritual battle. It's the moment you stop letting fear drive the car, and you put your hands back on the wheel.

Joseph Campbell noticed something strange and consistent across myths. Monsters tend to appear at the exact moments a hero is about to change, right before the breakthrough.

Which makes perfect sense, because in real life, that's when the monsters show up, too.

Not with fangs and claws. Sadly.

But with spreadsheets. With doom scrolling.

Monsters usually show up when you're close to something that matters. Something vulnerable. Something that might fail. Or worse, something that might actually work and change your life.

THE MONSTER'S FAVORITE DISGUISE

Procrastination is an emotion-regulation monster.

There's a point in every creative journey where you're staring at the blank page, the empty canvas, or the half-built project on your desk, and something invisible presses down on you.

You know you should move forward, but instead you find yourself cleaning the kitchen, reorganizing files, or falling into the bottomless scroll of the internet.

That invisible something? Meet your monster.

I've met dozens of mine over the years. Sometimes they showed up as cynicism ("This project is beneath you"). Other times, as perfectionism ("It's not ready yet. You're not ready yet."). I've battled the Fear of Not Being Original Monster, the Comparison Kraken, and the Deadline Dragon. They've all taken their turns slowing me down.

Here's what's most important to remember:

The monster isn't always your enemy. Sometimes it's a misguided bodyguard.

MEET THE MESSENGER

Every monster is also trying, in their own flawed way, to protect you.

The Perfectionist Pixie reminds you that you care deeply about your craft.

The Comparison Kraken shows you're hungry to grow.

Even the Cynicism Cyclops tries to save you from embarrassment.

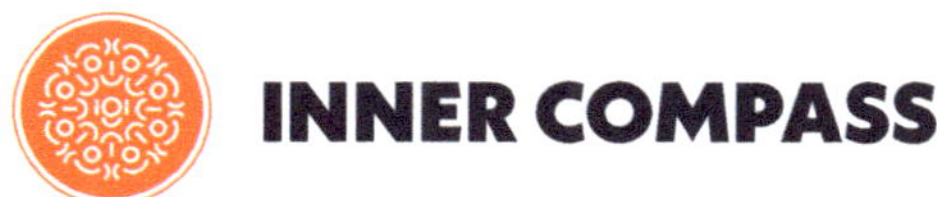

When you ask a monster, "What are you trying to protect me from?" you often discover it's not malicious. It's just misguided.

TRANSFORM THE RELATIONSHIP

Once you've met the messenger inside the monster, you can renegotiate your relationship.

Have a conversation with it. "Thanks for caring about my reputation, Cyclops, but I've got this."

Give it a smaller job. "Pixie, you can proofread after I finish the first draft. Not before."

Invite it to collaborate. "Kraken, you can suggest ways to make this better, but you don't get to stop me from starting."

After you name it, give it a face and a silly backstory. Turn it into a cartoon villain you can laugh at instead of an invisible force that runs your life.

The key is not to defeat the monster, but to work with it. Keep the wisdom and lose the paralysis. When you show up honestly, weird, earnest, fully you, the monsters lose their grip.

NAME THE MONSTER

Our weirdness and sincerity are often held hostage by monsters that thrive in the shadows. The fastest way to shrink them is to drag them into the light.

SOME COMMON MONSTERS I'VE SEEN IN WORKSHOPS I'VE HOSTED:

The first step in dealing with a monster is to call it by name. This makes it real, tangible, and therefore less powerful.

Deadline Dragon.

Breathing fire over your calendar until you panic and freeze.

Comparison Kraken.

Tangling you in the tentacles of "Why bother? They've already done it better."

Perfectionist Pixie.

Whispering that if it's not flawless, it's worthless.

Cynicism Cyclops

Rolling its single eye whenever you try something earnest.

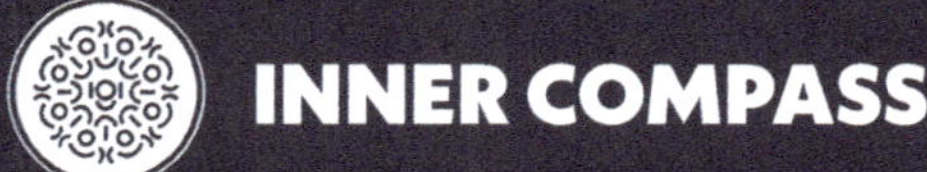

If your block is vague and formless, it can spread into every part of your creative life. Once you say, "I'm dealing with the Cynicism Cyclops," you can picture it. One glaring eye, maybe wearing a too-cool leather jacket. Then you can talk to it.

WHAT MONSTERS REALLY DO

Monsters are protectors with terrible communication skills. They keep you safe by keeping you small.

THEY'RE TRYING TO KEEP YOU SAFE FROM:

- Embarrassment
- Rejection
- Failure
- Disappointment
- Being seen
- Change

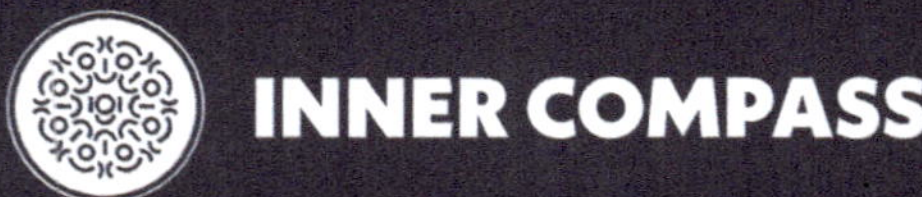

MONSTER STEPS

**This exercise helps you see your monsters clearly, learn from them,
and take back your power.**

1	**DRAW IT**	Give your monster form. Sketch it, doodle it, describe it.
2	**NAME IT**	Call your monster by a name. It could be literal ("Procrastination"), playful ("Sir Talks-a-Lot"), or dramatic ("The Fear of Failing Again").
3	**ASK WHAT IT'S PROTECTING**	Every monster is a guard dog for something. Ask: What is this monster trying to protect me from?
4	**DECIDE IF YOU STILL NEED THAT PROTECTION**	Sometimes the guard dog is overprotective. Is this protection still serving you?
5	**TAKE ONE TINY STEP FORWARD**	Slay the monster with action. Choose something so small it's undeniable: Write one sentence. Make one sketch. Share one idea.

"

THE MONSTER ISN'T HERE TO RUIN YOU.

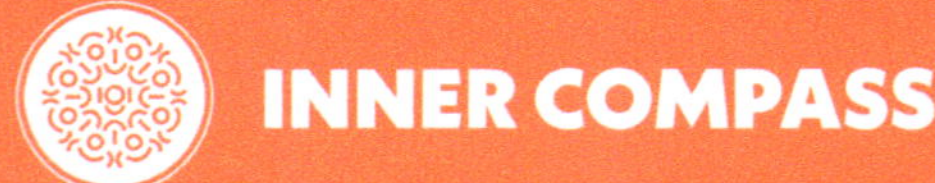

IT'S HERE TO REVEAL WHAT YOU CARE ABOUT, A BEACON POINTING STRAIGHT TOWARD YOUR DEEPEST VALUES.

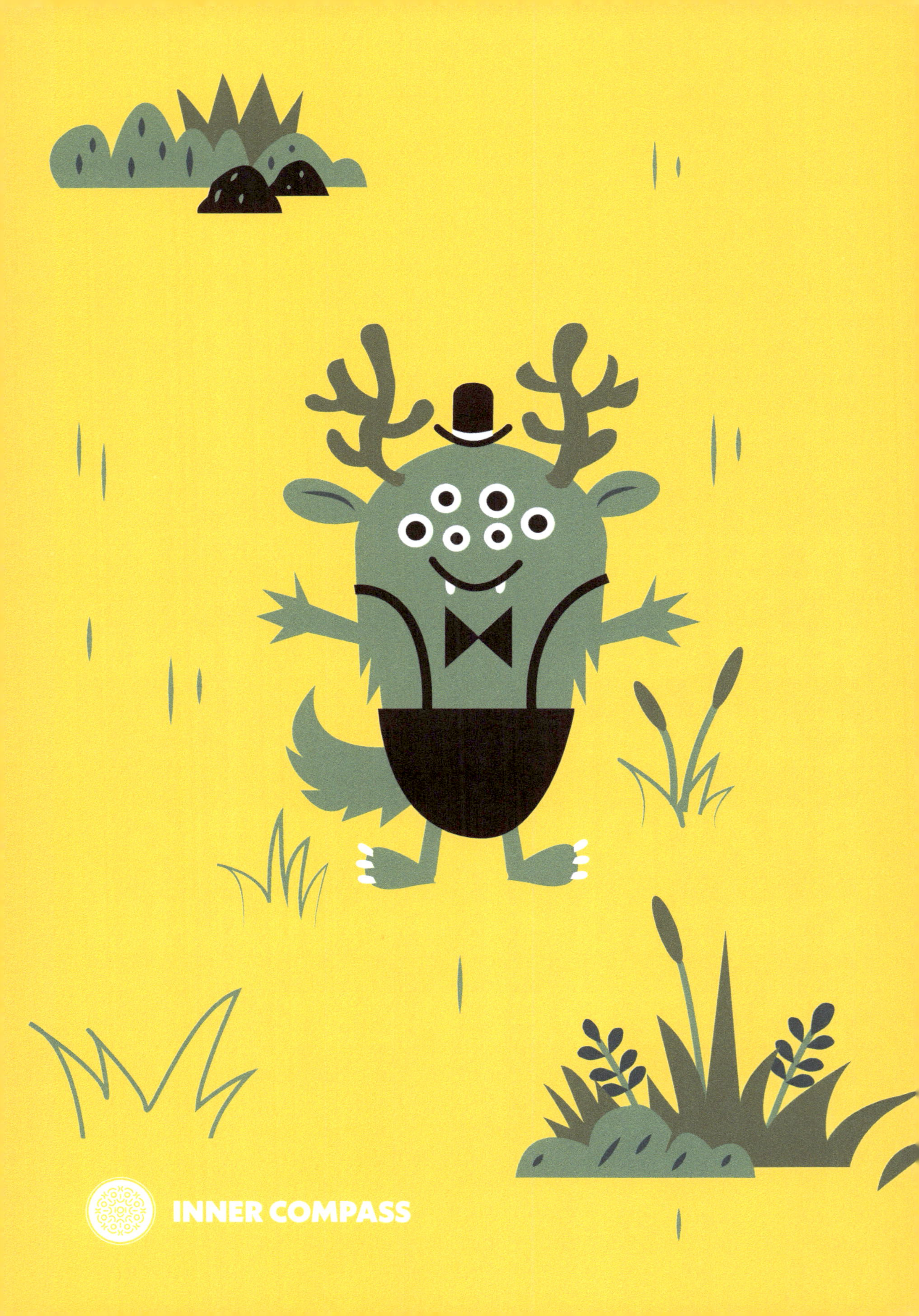

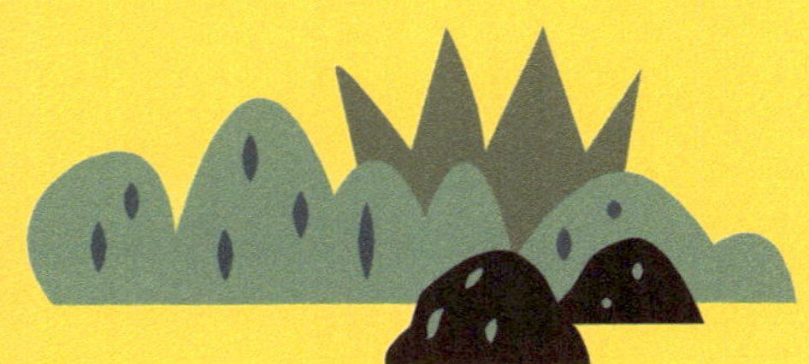
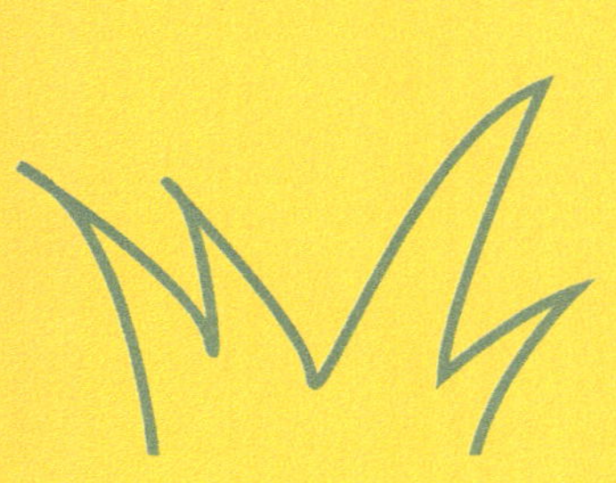
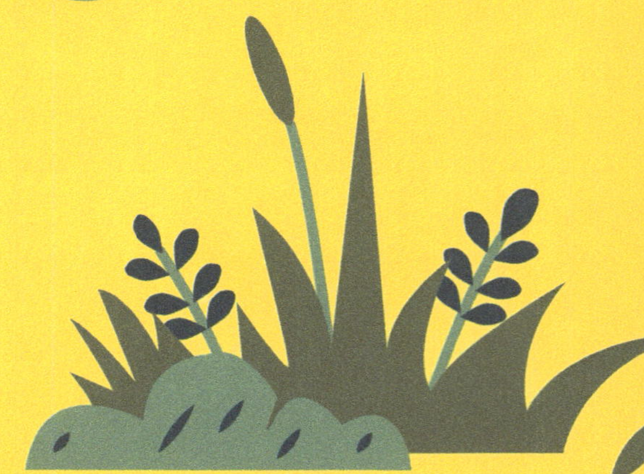

INNER COMPASS

CHAPTER 06

EMBRACE YOUR WEIRD
(WHY YOUR QUIRKS ARE YOUR CREATIVE SUPERPOWER)

Every creative era comes with a fork in the road.

One path is polished, normal, "professional." Sand down the edges. Keep the things that make you different from others tucked away where they can't embarrass you.

The other path is riskier: bring the weird with you.

Because the moment you decide to hide what makes you different is often the moment your best work starts disappearing.

THE BELLY OF THE WHALE

There's a stage in the Hero's Journey called the Belly of the Whale. It's the point where the hero has fully left the old world behind, but hasn't become the new version of themselves yet.

It looks like a pause from the outside, but it isn't defeat. It's a reflection.

This is the part of the journey where you stop trying to "win" through performance and approval, and start listening for what's real inside you. It's where the old identity dissolves, and something truer begins to form.

For a creative person, this is where you finally ask, *What do I love that I've been pretending not to love?*

MY BRAND OF WEIRD

Here's a very short list of what makes me different.

I make comic books. I collect dinosaur models. I have a not-so-small obsession with vintage blow-mold Halloween decorations. If you know, you know.

For a long time, I kept those quirks hidden. At work, I tried to fit in and sound like everyone else in meetings. I tried to make "clean" ideas that wouldn't raise eyebrows. I thought being professional meant being less…me.

When you hide your weirdness, you hide your best ideas.

You end up making safe work. Beige work. Work that could've come from anyone, and it will be forgotten by everyone.

The turning point came from the least corporate place imaginable, while hanging out with my kids.

I started teaching them how to make comics. The thing about kids is they don't care if you're cool. They care if you're real. They can smell fake enthusiasm like a shark smells a drop of blood.

So I stopped pretending and leaned into my joy for comics, monsters, and robots. The whole weird parade.

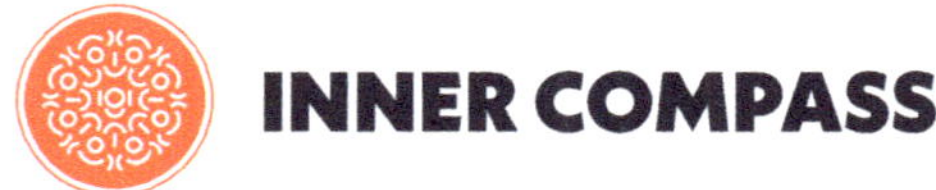

INNER COMPASS

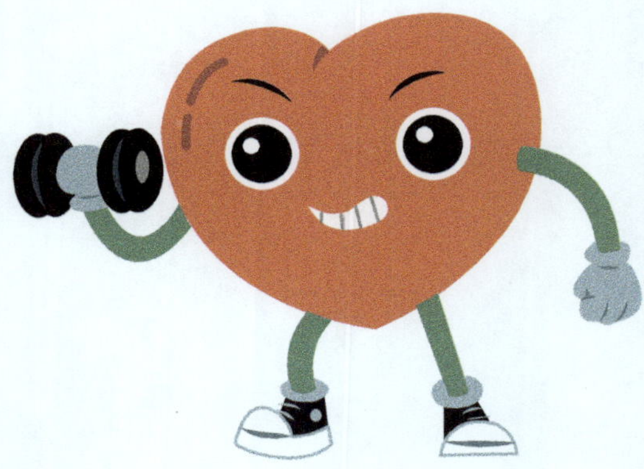

And they loved it.

Not long after that, I went to their school and asked if I could run a class for the third graders and teach the whole grade how to make their own comic books. I built a simple curriculum that helped them make it their own.

Every kid made something different and beautiful.

And later, I got nominated for "Special Person of the Year" by the PTA, all because I let my weird out of the box.

That's when it hit me. My weird wasn't the thing that made me less credible. It was the thing that made me an original.

THE ARMOR OF CYNICISM

There's a reason we hide our weird. Hiding feels safer.

For years, I wore cynicism like armor.

If I laughed at things first, nobody could laugh at me. If I stayed detached, I couldn't be disappointed. If I acted like I didn't care, I couldn't get hurt.

It worked in the short term. It cost me everything in the long term because cynicism keeps you at a distance from other people, joy, and your own heart.

It makes you feel invulnerable, but it also makes you unreachable.

And what was unveiled under that armor was sincerity and courage. Caring out loud even when you know you might get laughed at. It's saying, "Yes, I love this thing," and letting that love shape your work.

WEIRD AS AN ASSET

For years, I thought my quirks were flaws.

The colors I loved were "too loud."

My ideas were "too playful."

References were "too niche."

Some people have brains that catch more "random" signals. They notice odd connections or pick up strange gems. That can make you feel weird when you're young.

However, if you keep going, it's often what makes you valuable.

In the Belly of the Whale, I learned that clients, collaborators, and audiences don't fall in love with safe ideas. They fall in love with a voice, which lives in the

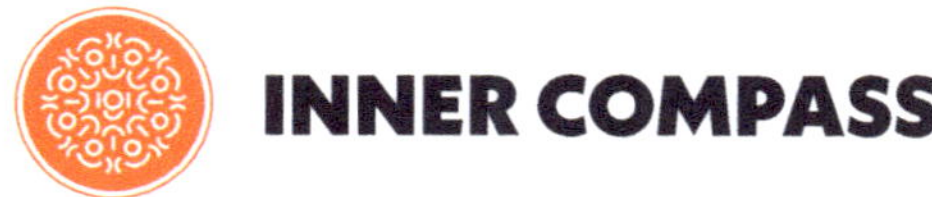

weird, in those oddly specific preferences, obsessions, and angles that only you can bring.

WHY WEIRD WINS

Your weirdness is your fingerprint.

The world doesn't need more safe, copycat work. Your sincerity is the oxygen that lets your creative work breathe. Together, they develop your creative superpower.

So embrace your weird.

Wear it proudly. Teach it to your kids. Offer it to your team. Build a life where you don't have to hide the parts of you that contain the magic because that's exactly what makes you unforgettable.

YOUR QUIRKS ARE YOUR ADVANTAGE. The loves and obsessions of your childhood are a blueprint for your most original work.

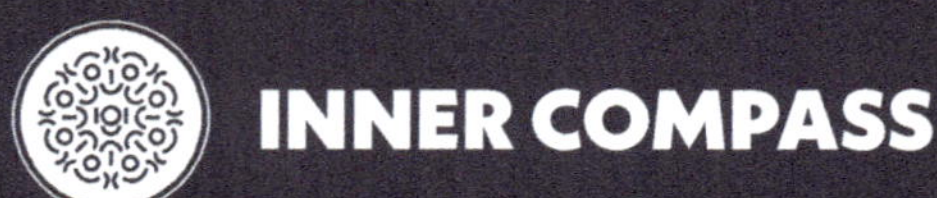

"
IF CREATIVITY
IS THE SIGNAL,
WEIRDNESS IS THE
FREQUENCY THAT
CUTS THROUGH
THE NOISE.

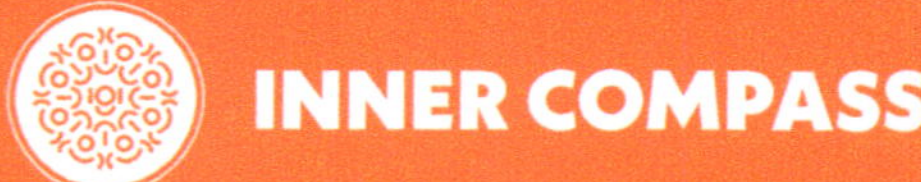
INNER COMPASS

IT'S THE HUMAN GLITCH AI CAN'T FAKE BECAUSE IT'S ROOTED IN OBSESSION AND LIVED EXPERIENCE.

MAD SKILLS

As you begin your descent, the return flight can get bumpy. Fear not, my young apprentice. We're about to stack the wins, build your super-robot team, mine your early loves, and return with the elixir.

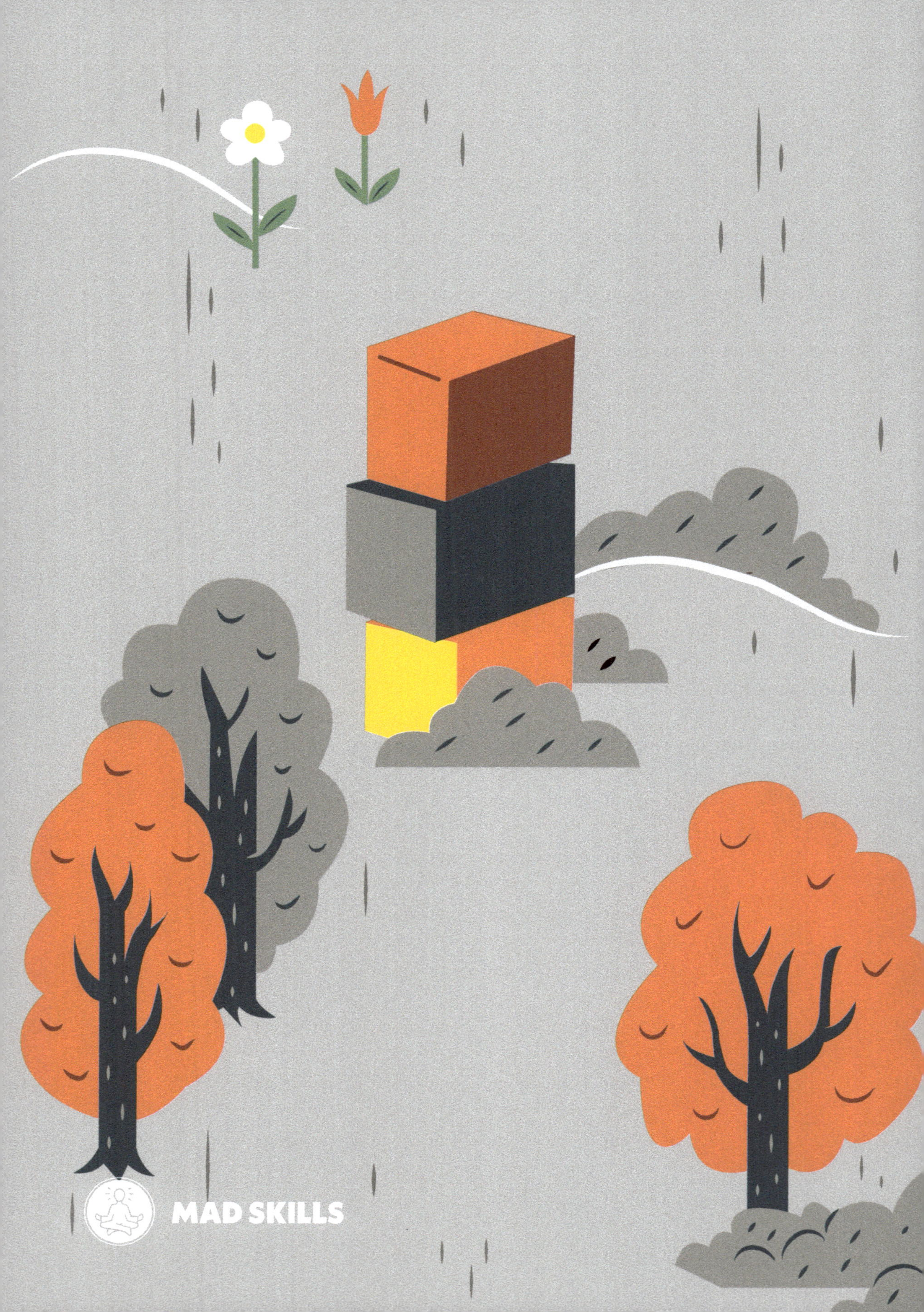
MAD SKILLS

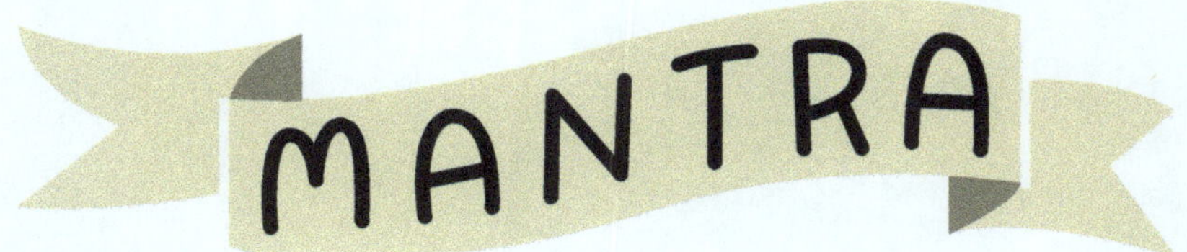

CHAPTER 07

STACK THE WINS: THE POWER OF SMALL BEGINNINGS

Big dreams are beautiful. They are also…BIG. Sometimes so large they make your brain freeze, the classic survival move.

When the gap between where you are and where you want to be feels like a canyon, your mind starts negotiating.

"I'll start when I have more time."

"I'll start when I feel inspired."

"I'll start when I'm ready."

Creativity only thrives in motion. That's why we need to stack the wins.

A small win feels like more than a consolation prize. It's a spark. It's proof of the simplest possible signal to your nervous system that says: We're moving. We're not stuck.

In Hero's Journey terms, this is the next step for surviving the Road of Trials and the string of manageable skirmishes.

WHEN THE COMPASS FELT BROKEN

In 2020, my family and I moved to Oregon. It was supposed to be an adventure in a new city with a new school, new friends, and new energy.

Instead, we landed in a global lockdown.

We were isolated, drained, and miserable. Our whole family felt like the internal compass that usually points toward "what's next" was just spinning in circles.

One night at the dinner table, we decided to try something different.

We would start collecting tiny wins we could actually control. Something small that proves today wasn't a total loss.

So we started a list.

We went to the community pool.

We tried new hiking trails.

We found local waterfalls.

We made a point to meet people and build community.

The kids volunteered.

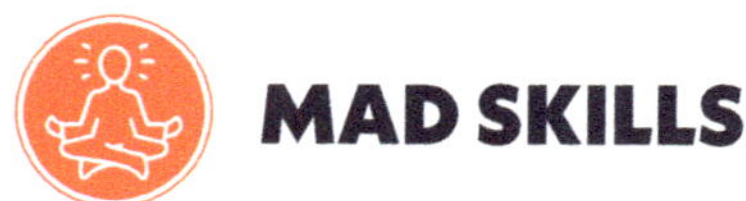

We tried new hobbies.

By the end of the summer, the list itself had become medicine. We could see we were building a life again. We weren't waiting to feel better. We were doing small things that made feeling "better" possible.

That's what win-stacking does. It turns "stuck" into "in motion."

WHY SMALL BEGINNINGS MATTER

Small beginnings lead to great adventures. They're how you weather the trials and tribulations of a creative life. When you hit obstacles, doubt, burnout, or the "this is too big" moments, small actions are what pull you through.

Instead of asking, "How do I finish the whole project?" ask:

What is one win I can earn today?

Write 100 words.

Sketch one page.

Share one post.

Build one tiny prototype.

Start small, but start often. The compounding power of consistent action creates a hundred small wins that can move mountains.

And keep track. Record your wins somewhere you can see them because once you can see the wins stacking up, the invisible becomes visible.

WHY STACKING SMALL WINS WORKS

This is not just motivational poster logic. Your brain is built for this.

Small wins create momentum. When you complete something, your brain gets a little reward signal, which makes it easier to take the next step. (This is why "start with one tiny thing" works so annoyingly well.)

Progress is a powerful motivator. You do not need a life overhaul to feel alive again. You need evidence that you are moving.

Small wins reshape your identity. Every time you follow through, you're not just finishing a task. You're casting a vote for the kind of person you are, someone who shows up.

Incremental change beats heroic bursts. The steady path is the sustainable path. Small improvements compound into large outcomes.

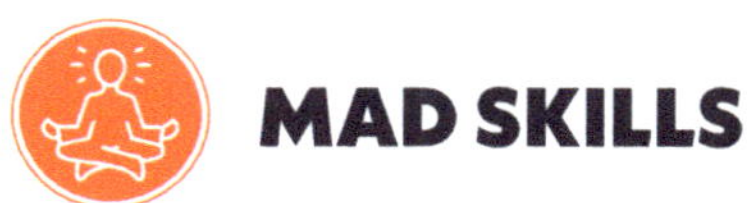

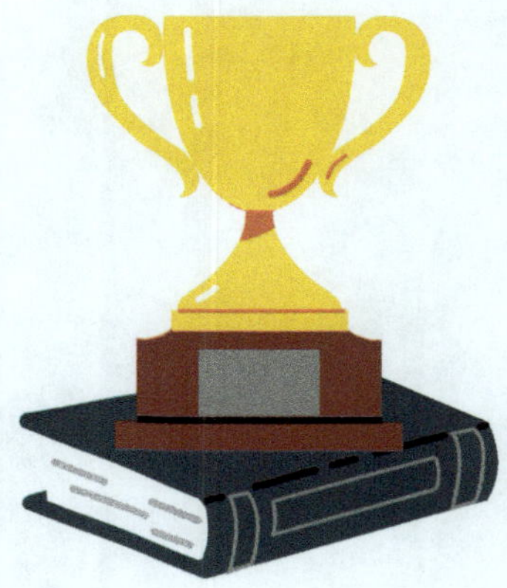

HOW TO START STACKING

Lower the bar. Choose a task so small it's almost ridiculous: write one sentence, sketch one shape, tidy one corner of your desk.

Use habit stacking. Attach a new win to something you already do: after you pour your coffee, write one line.

Track and celebrate. A checkmark counts. A note counts. A running list counts. The point is to make progress visible.

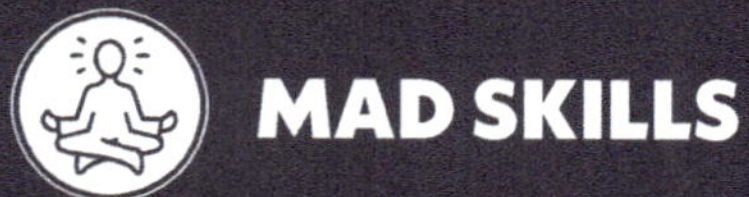

MAD SKILLS

START A "10 WINS" LIST

Brainstorm ten simple wins you could complete this week.

1	**CHOOSE 1–3 AND DO THEM**	Today if possible
2	**TRACK THEM SOMEWHERE VISIBLE**	Notebook/whiteboard
3	**WATCH YOUR MOMENTUM STACK**	Anchor a Reflection

CREATIVE	**PHYSICAL**	**RELATIONAL**
(sketch, draft, brainstorm)	(walk, stretch, tidy workspace)	(send thank-you, share an idea)

" BIG CHANGE

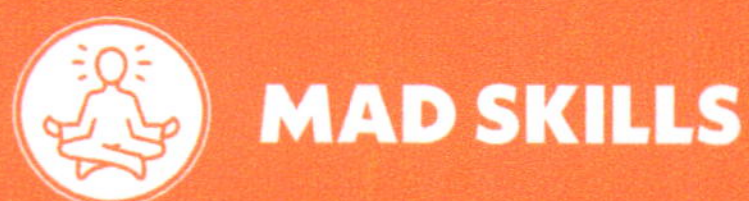

IS JUST SMALL WINS, STACKED.

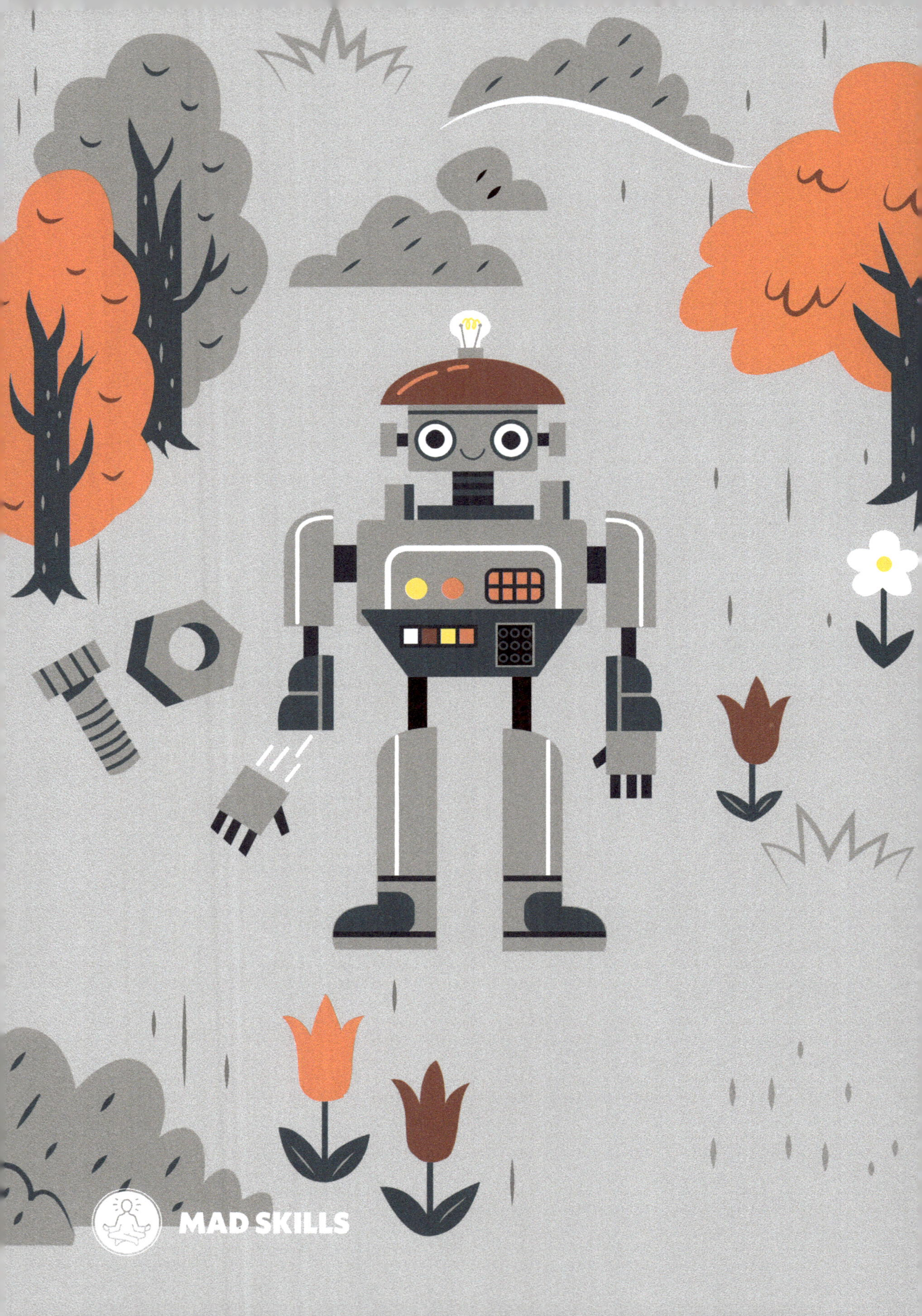
MAD SKILLS

CHAPTER 08

BUILD YOUR CREATIVE SUPER-ROBOT

In a creative career, you'll cross paths with many kinds of people. Some will be talented. Some will be wildly talented. Some will be the rare combination: wildly talented and oddly-shaped enough to fit perfectly into your personal super-robot schematic.

This is where the magic happens.

A lot of people feel threatened when they meet someone who seems to outshine them.

Have you ever thought, "They're better than me. They could replace me."?

That's your ego trying to keep you safe by keeping you small. Ignore it.

Surrounding yourself with people who are smarter, faster, or more skilled than you is not a risk. It's an advantage. They keep you humble and inspired. They pull you upwards.

WHY IT MATTERS

Creative work thrives in community. Great collaborators don't replace you. They expand you. Iron sharpens iron, and creative greatness is contagious if you let it be. The goal is to build the kind of room where better work becomes inevitable.

Your allies make the impossible possible. They push you when you're stuck, protect you from burnout, and celebrate wins in a way only another creator can understand.

Build your team like you're assembling the most glorious, weird, powerful machine in the world.

BLUEPRINT FOR YOUR SUPER-ROBOT

Think of your creative life as a Voltron you're assembling over time. You don't need one perfect "dream team."

The Core Processor – The Mentor

This is your Obi-Wan or Gandalf. They don't fight for you, but they help you think clearly and choose the right road when everything feels foggy.

Real-life equivalent:

a career mentor, wise elder, teacher, or coach.

The Heavy Armor – The Protectors

These people keep your chassis intact. When you fail (and every hero does), they make sure the damage isn't permanent. They remind you you're loved even when your work is messy.

Real-life equivalent:

family, old friends, your partner, your "no matter what" people.

The Radar/ Sensors – The Truth-Tellers

A robot is useless if its sensors are calibrated wrong. You need people who will tell you with love when you're being arrogant, avoidant, lazy, or delusional.

Real-life equivalent:

one brutally honest friend, a peer who gives real feedback, someone who can do radical candor without cruelty.

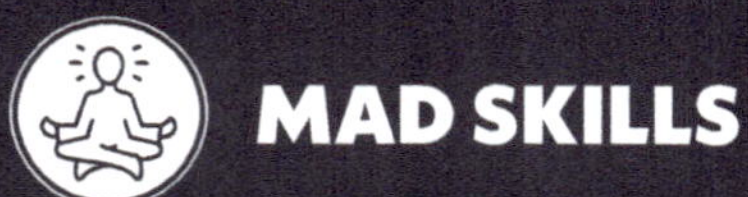

You need a few key parts that keep you moving, learning, and protected.

The Power Source – The Energizers

Every journey needs fuel. These allies believe in the mission even when your battery is at 1%. They remind you that your work matters when you've forgotten.

Real-life equivalent:

your biggest fans, your creative community, a hype-friend, a "gym buddy," your Workbench people.

The Specialized Tools – The Experts

Sometimes you need a specific skill you don't have time to learn. The pro who can do the thing cleanly so you can stay in your zone of genius.

Real-life equivalent:

accountant, therapist, producer, developer, lawyer, editor, tech-wizard coworker.

BUILD YOUR TEAM FROM DIFFERENCE, NOT DUPLICATION.

The best creative machine is made of people who bring something you do not.

08

YOUR ALLIES ARE OUT THERE. Go find them and build something bigger than you could alone.

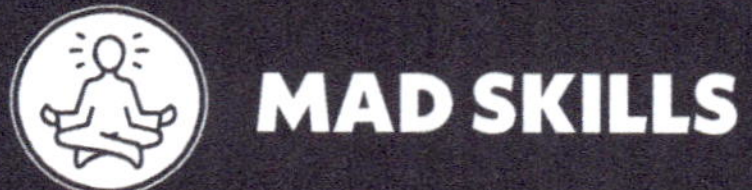

DRAW YOUR SUPER-ROBOT

Your best work is rarely built alone.
Draw the people, habits, and forces that power your creative machine.

1	**GRAB A BLANK PAGE**	Draw a simple robot with a head, two arms, and two legs.
2	**ASSIGN**	Each part a skill, trait, or role you don't have but wish you did.
3	**WRITE DOWN**	The names of people you know who could fill those rolesor describe your dream collaborator.
4	**PICK ONE ROLE**	Reach out to that person this week. Start a conversation, share an idea, or invite them into your creative world.

" GEAR UP, SUPER-ROBOT.

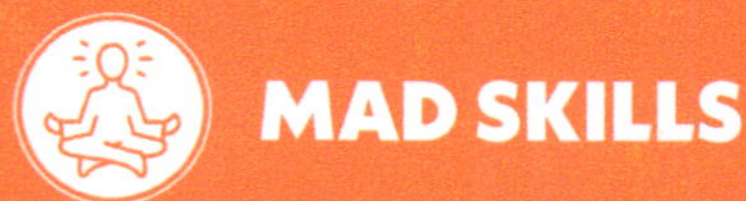

TECH-FORCE, UNITE!

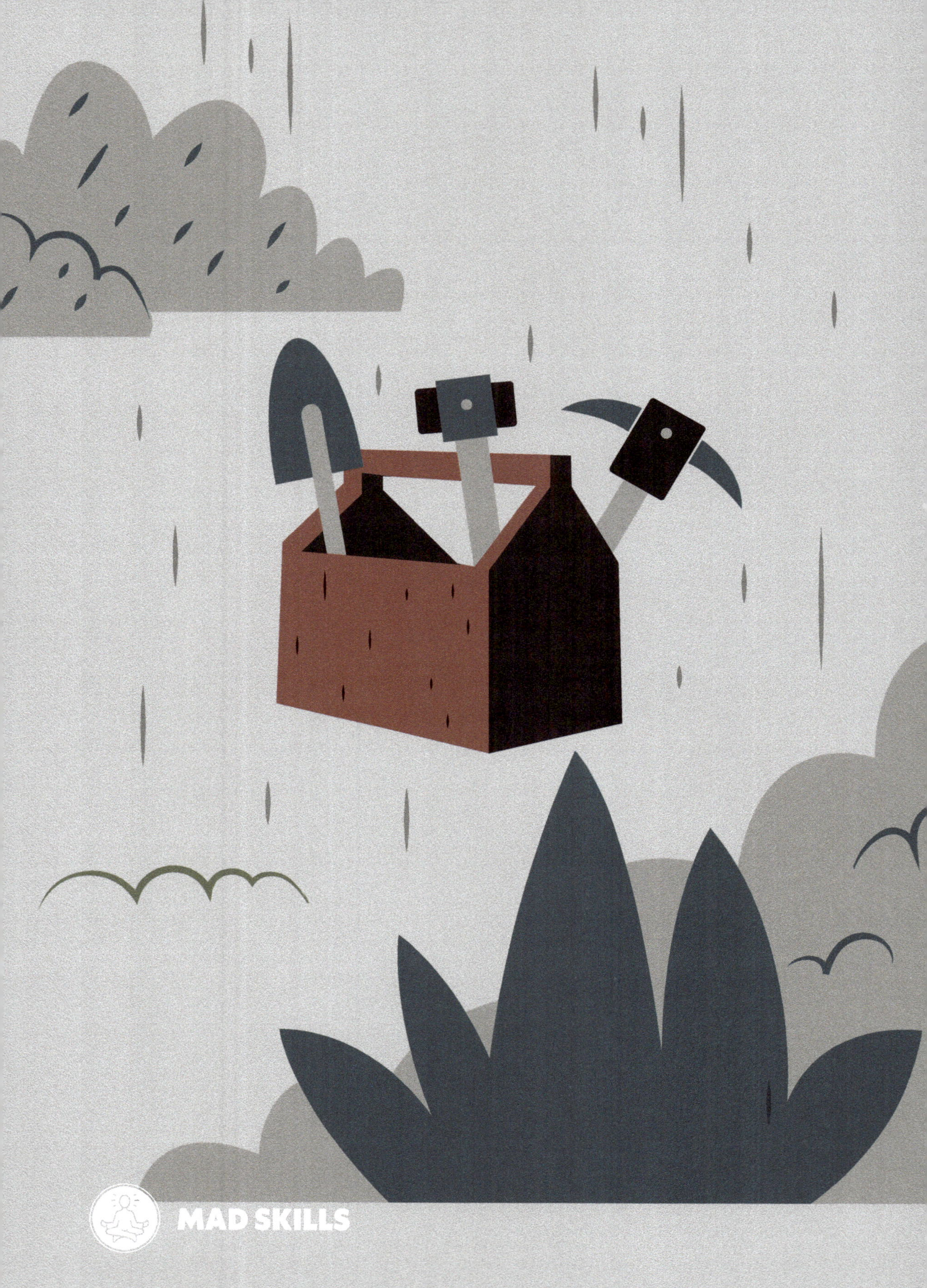
MAD SKILLS

CHAPTER 09

MINING EARLY LOVES: CARING FIERCELY, CREATING JOYFULLY

You remember my robot story from the beginning, right?

I grew up loving robots, got a really cool job where I pitched them this awesome robot idea, and it went over like that *Godzilla* movie in the 90s. Which is to say, it DIED.

So later, I'm the creative director at a start-up, and they're looking for a similar kind of thing. A way to express the brand in fun, interesting ways, so I start digging around the archives, and what do I find?

They have an old illustration of a robot named Otto.

Initiate robot superpower!

So I got to work and poured everything into this pitch, which means it had all the childhood-level passion I have for robots and all the adult skills I've learned the hard way.

Instead of making a normal PowerPoint, I made it a comic book with a whole backstory for this robot named Otto. Just like the comics I read when I was a kid.

(Or the comics I read last Wednesday, for that matter.)

I pitched it to my boss. This time, my robot flew.

Not only did they buy it, they went all in. They explained they had been expressing the brand through Otto, and our team got to do the kind of work that makes you remember why you chose this career in the first place.

Otto has been a comic book, web banners, pins, stickers, and sales materials. We made toys and brick-style builds. We even built a life-size Otto and had him guard the booth at conferences like a friendly robot bouncer.

I had the time of my life because I'm getting to combine my deep, early loves with real, hard-earned craft. That combination is rocket fuel.

THE TRICK YOU'RE REALLY LEARNING

A creative professional learns how to mine their early loves for inspiration and passion.

That does not mean you live in nostalgia forever. It means you learn where your creative energy originates, and you bring those raw materials forward into your work today.

Early loves are your first creative language. The characters, moods, colors, obsessions, and story-shapes that made your imagination spark before you started worrying about being cool, realistic, or "serious" about your work.

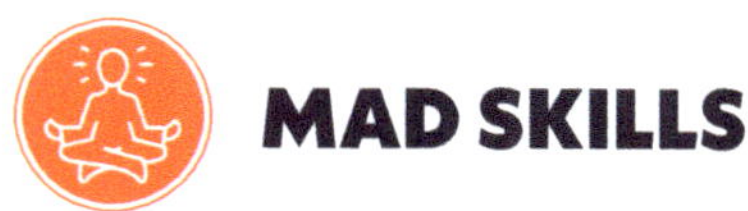

Those early loves become your creative DNA.

When you bring them forward into your work today, your creativity feels more joyful and unmistakably yours.

THE WORK BENEATH THE WORK

A lot of people think creativity comes from chasing new ideas.

In the Hero's Journey, sometimes it does. But a surprising amount of your best work comes from combining what you already love with what you've learned.

That's what mining early loves really means.

You are going back to the source and bringing back materials that still contain power.

Think of it like a simple formula:

Early Love + Adult Skill = Personal Magic

That's the Otto recipe. And it works for way more than robots.

WHAT I LOVE

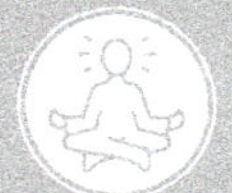

WHY THIS MATTERS IN A CYNICAL WORLD

Creative work is, at its core, an act of hope. It requires us to believe in something that doesn't exist yet and to commit to bringing it into reality. That belief is fragile.

Cynicism, whether it comes from other people or from the little voice in your own head, can erode hope before the work even begins.

Mining your early loves is defensive magic, a way to protect your creative spark from the part of you that wants to roll its eyes, play it safe, and stay unhurt. Then you create work that no one else could make, because no one else has your exact recipe of obsessions, influences, scars, and delights.

INSIGHT
09
CREATIVITY ECHOES OUTWARD. Mapping your legacy shows
how your work will ripple into the future.

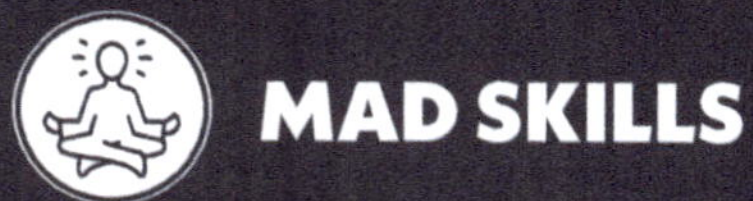
MAD SKILLS

CREATIVE LEGACY MAP

A map to connect your past, present, and future contributions.

1	**PAST MILESTONES**	3–5 creative milestones that shaped you.
2	**PRESENT CONTRIBUTIONS**	List the creative work you're doing now.
3	**FUTURE GOALS**	3–5 goals, dreams, or projects you'd like to be remembered for.
4	**DRAW YOUR MAP**	Sketch your legacy map.
5	**REFLECTION**	What themes connect your past, present, and future?

"

WHAT LIT YOU UP AS A CHILD

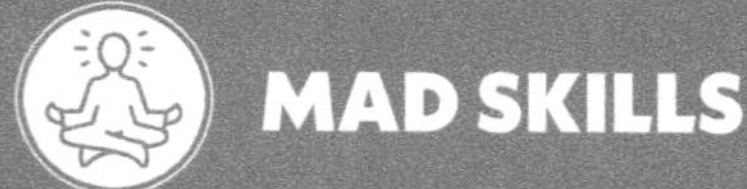

IS A MAP TO WHAT YOU'RE MEANT TO BUILD.

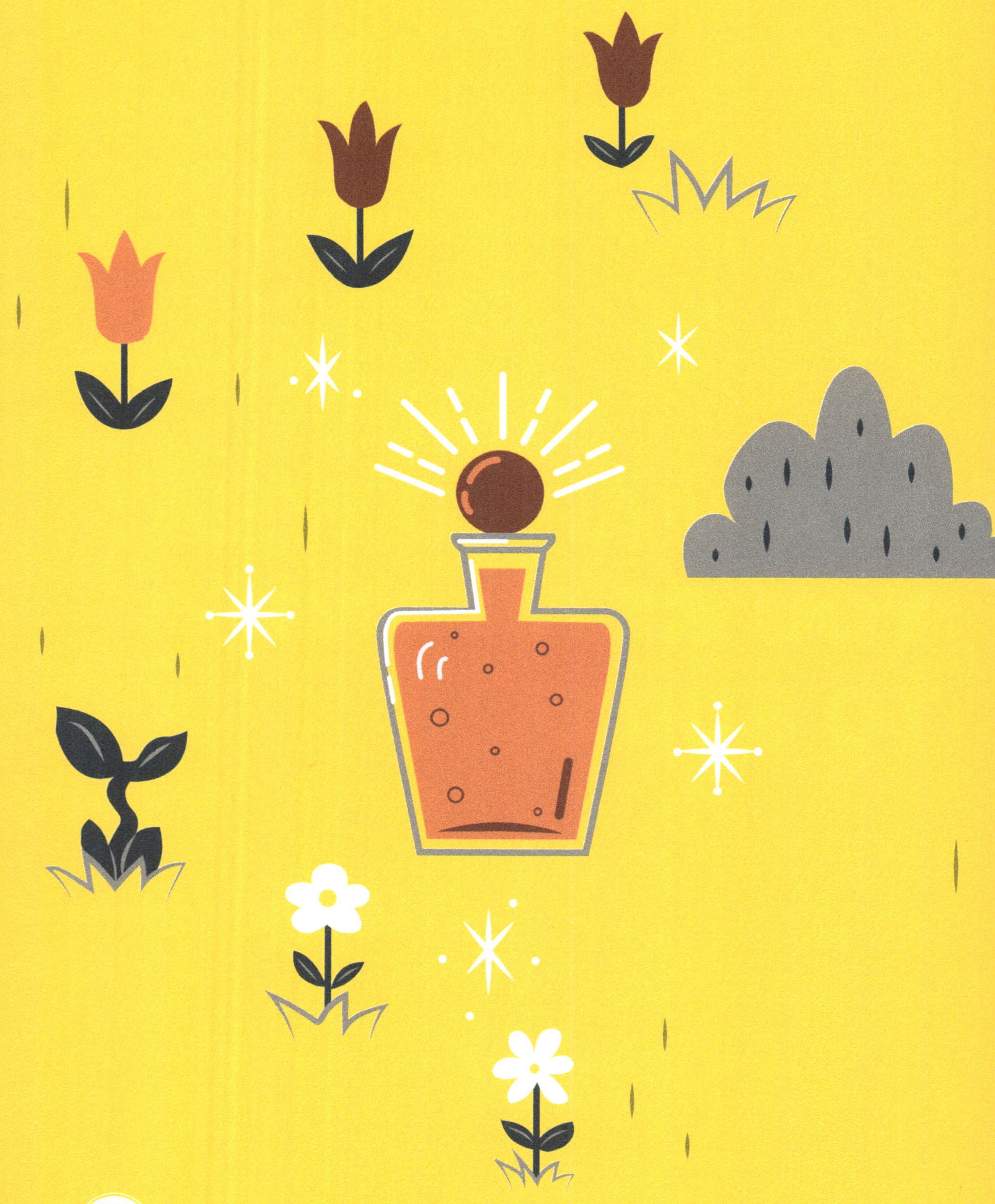
MAD SKILLS

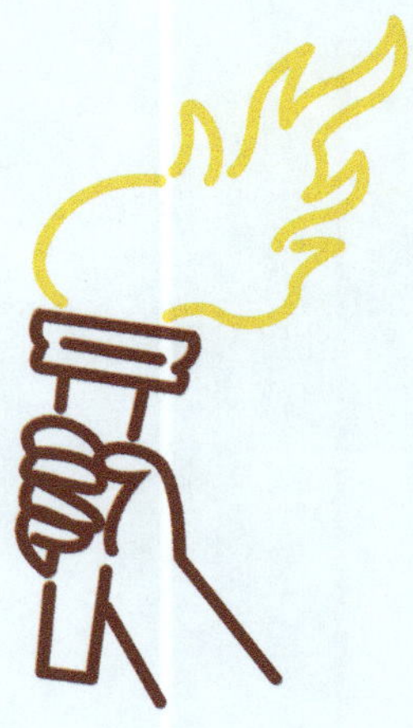

CHAPTER 10

RETURN WITH THE ELIXIR: BRINGING THE TREASURE HOME

If you've ever watched *Star Wars, The Lion King,* or any great adventure story, you've seen the pattern: the hero leaves home, faces trials, discovers allies, defeats monsters, and returns with something valuable, such as wisdom, healing, treasure, or just a story that changes everything.

This is more than a formula for a great story; it's the formula for life. It's your creative formula, too.

You've left familiar shores before, the job you outgrew, the city that no longer fit, the comfort zone you finally stepped out of. You faced monsters (hello, perfectionism and procrastination), found allies (your super-robot team), and stumbled into surprising wins (remember to stack them). Each time, you brought something back: a story, a lesson, a piece of yourself you didn't know you had.

The question now is: What are you going to do with it?

Have no fear. You are now at the stage where, to be the hero, you have to bring the elixir (the Mad Skills) back to help others.

MY FORTY-EIGHT JOBS AND COUNTING

At last count, I've had forty-eight jobs. By the time you read this, I might be on job forty-nine. Each one was its own mini-adventure, some were detours, some were disasters, some were absolute gifts. The pattern was always the same, though: leave, learn, return with something worth carrying forward.

Every era gave me an elixir. Pixar® taught me that sincerity matters more than polish. Duarte taught me that storytelling can change business. Automox taught me to mine my early loves and let robots and monsters back into the room. Even the layoffs and flops taught me resilience.

And the best part? Sharing those elixirs multiplies their value. That's why I teach, write, and even why I'm handing you this book.

The Map of Your Eras

Think back on your own story. Can you see the eras? The Bigger Dreams, the Inner Compass, the Mad Skills? The jobs, relationships, or projects that defined a chapter of your life?

Each era left you with something: a scar or skill, maybe a friendship or a truth. That's your elixir. The moment you share it, in your work, community, or family, it becomes a legacy.

Try This: grab your notebook and draw a timeline.

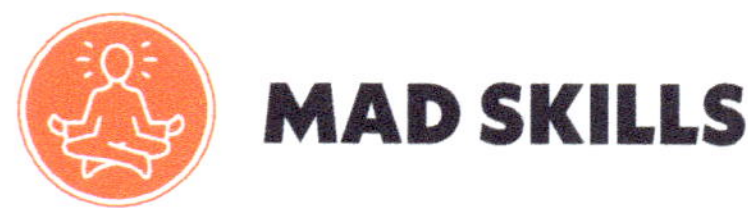

Divide it into three sections:

1. **Bigger Dreams:** your early leaps, wild risks, or bold beginnings.

2. **Inner Compass:** When you started listening to joy, sincerity, or your own weirdness.

3. **Mad Skills:** when you sharpened your craft, found allies, and began to give back.

Under each, jot the key events, monsters, mentors, and wins. Then write the elixir you carried out of that era. What lesson or gift did you bring back?

The end of the Hero's Journey isn't a castle or a throne. It's the chance to come home changed and offer your hard-won treasure to others.

That's the invitation of creativity—to make meaning from the things you create. To mine your weird, face your monsters, stack your wins, and then hand the prize inside to someone else.

Another era is waiting. Another adventure is calling. Take what you've learned here. Share it. Teach it. Shape it into work only you can do. Step into it with joy as your compass. Your creative life is more than what you make. It's the lives you change by sharing it.

10

THE GIFT OF CREATIVITY GROWS STRONGER WHEN SHARED.
Your elixir is meant to return to the world.

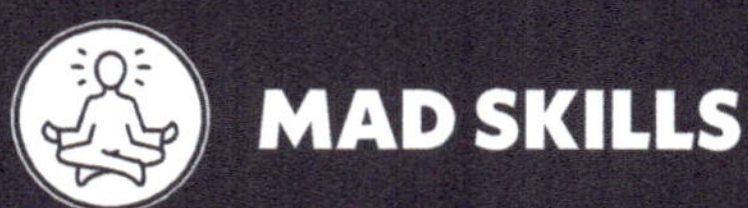

RETURN WITH THE ELIXIR

Every creative journey ends with bringing something back: an insight, a tool, a story.

1	NAME YOUR ELIXIR	What is the core treasure?
2	DEFINE HOW YOU'LL SHARE IT	List 1 way you can share it with a member of your robot team.
3	MAP YOUR CREATIVE LEGACY	Sketch or outline how your elixir might ripple outward over time.

GROWTH IS
A SOLO JOURNEY;

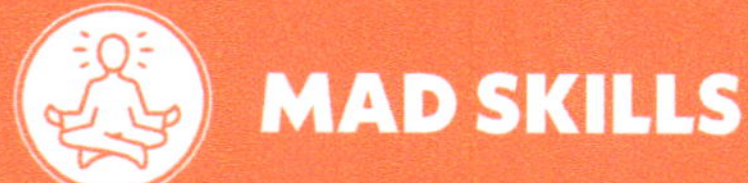

WISDOM IS A
SHARED RETURN.

CLOSING

THE FIELD GUIDE TO CREATIVITY: A COMPASS

If you've read this far, you've traveled with me through joy and monsters, robots and mentors, ponds and vision boards, wins both small and strange. You've seen how sincerity can slay cynicism, how weirdness becomes a superpower, and how creativity can move forward with your compass pointed toward joy.

This compass won't tell you exactly where to step, but it will always point you toward what matters most: joy, sincerity, weirdness, resilience, and connection. If you keep orienting yourself to those, you'll find your way.

WHAT TO CARRY FORWARD

JOY IS YOUR COMPASS.
When you lose it, you're off course. When you find it, you're home.

MENTORS MATTER.
Find yours. And when you can, be one for someone else.

VISION FUELS ACTION.
Don't just dream it: see it, build it, name it out loud.

EVERY POND HAS VALUE.
Swim where you can grow, and move when it's time.

WEIRD IS POWER.
Don't hide the quirks. They're the fingerprints of your creativity.

MONSTERS AREN'T THE ENEMY.
They're fear in disguise. Name them, laugh at them, keep moving.

WINS STACK.
Tiny steps turn into mountains you climb.

ALLIES BUILD THE ROBOT.
Find the people who make you stronger, and build together.

YOUR EARLY LOVES ARE A TREASURE.
Mine them. They're your most authentic fuel.

RETURN WITH THE ELIXIR AND SHARE WHAT YOU'VE LEARNED.
That's how your story becomes legacy.

THE NEXT ADVENTURE

As you set this book down, your next creative era is waiting. Maybe it's a bold leap. Maybe it's a quiet step. Maybe it's a monster you'll finally face, or a weird love you'll finally bring into the light.

Whatever it is, let this guide remind you that sincerity is strength, caring is rebellion, and creativity isn't about perfection.

Thank you for traveling with me. I can't wait to see what you create, and what elixirs you bring back to share.

ACKNOWLEDGMENTS

This book wouldn't exist without the many people who've walked beside me on my creative journey.

To my wife, Tarah, thank you for giving me the space, encouragement, and belief that my ideas were worth chasing. You've been my safe harbor and greatest adventure all at once.

To my creative allies, the collaborators, mentors, and friends who have shared their brilliance, challenged my thinking, and reminded me why the work matters. I'm endlessly grateful.

To my kids, thank you for inspiring me daily, reminding me that imagination is limitless, and joining me in the joyful mess of making things. You helped me see the beauty of embracing your own brand of weird.

To my mom, dad, and sister, thank you for surviving my early years and for loving, encouraging, and supporting me through all of it. I would not be here without you.

To the wildly talented teams I've been fortunate to lead and learn from, your dedication, courage, and camaraderie shaped my vision for what creative leadership can be.

To my friend, Doug Neff, thank you for helping me write, craft, and organize all these ideas. Your steady guidance, sharp questions, and generous spirit turned a mountain of notes into a clear path. I'm grateful for your partnership and your belief in this project.

To my friend Ryan O'Rourke, your beautiful illustrations truly bring this book to life. Thank you. You are one of the great reasons graduate school paid off.

And finally, to the reader, thank you for picking up this guide, for trusting me to walk with you through your own creative era. My hope is that you leave these pages with more courage, curiosity, and a reminder that the world needs exactly what only you can create.

KEEP GOING AFTER THE TRAIL ENDS.

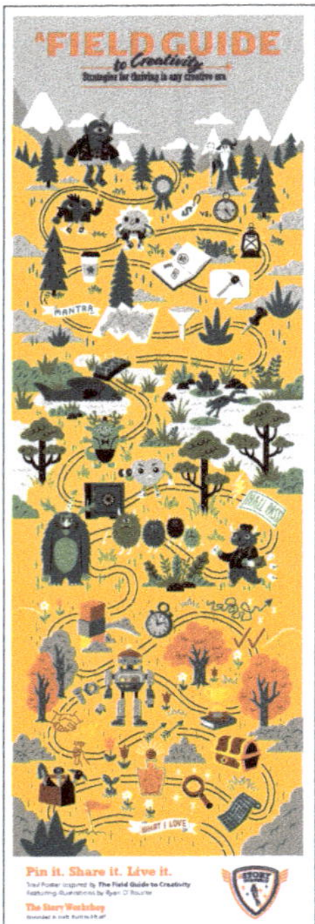

Visit **thestoryworkshop.com**, sign up for the newsletter, and I'll send you a free **Field Guide** poster to help keep your creativity moving in the right direction.

ABOUT THE AUTHOR

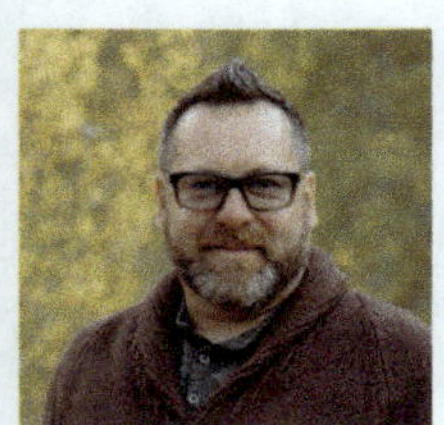

Erik has always created. From films, books, and magazines to scripts, comics, and children's stories, he has built narratives that move people. With more than twenty years in creative leadership, Erik has created work for top-tier brands like Pixar®, Facebook™, Cisco®, Salesforce®, and ServiceNow®, at agencies and independently.

Equally at home in startups and global teams, Erik thrives in fast-paced, idea-rich environments. He leads with vision, mentors with passion, and builds teams that deliver. His foundation in animation, illustration, branding, and design allows him to craft work that connects deeply, visually, and conceptually.

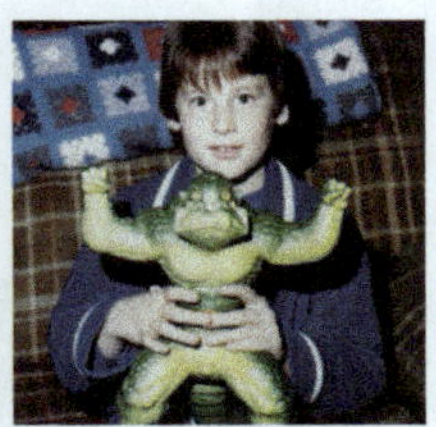

When not leading creative initiatives for others, Erik is in the studio drawing, building, and dreaming.

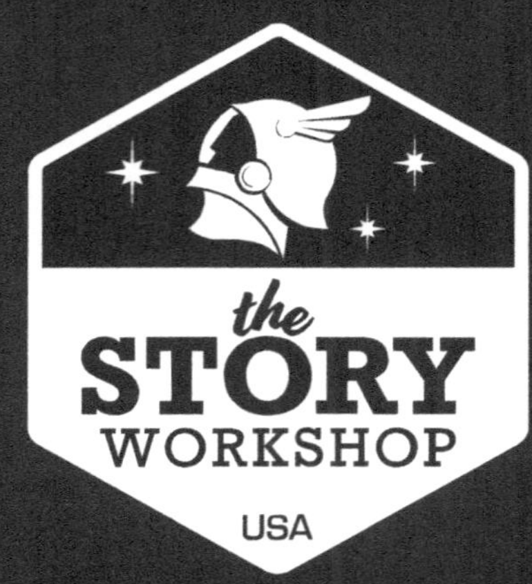

www.thestoryworkshop.com